H

MW01288600

Written by:

Brahma Kumari Pari

Edited and improved upon by:

Shiv Baba Service Initiative

(a BK team dedicated in doing Godly
service)

TABLE OF CONTENTS

INTRODUCTION

A human mind thinks approximately 60,000 to 70,000 thoughts per day; out of this 90% goes waste. Most of these thoughts are generated automatically to bring about a continuous flow of thoughts in the mind. Since we are usually not paying attention to these thoughts, we may not be aware that numerous thoughts are streaming through our mind. The creation of these thoughts is inspired by what we see and hear during the day.

What we think in the mind is reflected in our words and karma/actions, and it leads to the formation of habits. Our collection of karma, and habits, create our destiny. For this reason, we should be more careful of what we think.

Have you ever tried to check your thoughts? We are hardly conscious of our thoughts and, generally, we do not monitor the way we think. If we become aware of how we think, we can check our thoughts and change it; if we can change our thoughts we can change our destiny. This book will guide you on "How to Think" based on the Murli (God's teachings) of Brahma Kumaris Godly Spiritual University.

The knowledge in the Murli (hereafter also referred to as the 'BK knowledge') is used by the members of the Brahma Kumaris to create elevated thoughts. Through just one powerful elevated thought, you will be in the Angelic World with God (Shiv Baba).

Before 1969, the Murli was given through using the physical body of Brahma Baba. After Brahma Baba left his physical body, in 1969, the Murli was given through the physical body of Dadi Gulzar. The Murli, which was spoken by God through using the physical body of Brahma Baba, is called 'Sakar Murli'. The Murli, which was spoken through Dadi Gulzar, is referred to as the Avyakt Murli.

This book has been written to guide the readers to only think about the knowledge that is given by God in the Murlis. Thinking about this Godly knowledge will make you spiritually powerful. Hence, there are extracts from the Murlis, in this book, along with some explanations and suggestions. The date, when the Murli was read in the BK centers, is given at the top of each murli extract. 'SM' stands for Sakar Murli and 'AM' refers to the Avyakt Murli.

The explanations given, after each murli extract, will help you to understand what God is saying in the relevant Murli. So you will find it easier to churn (think about/contemplate on) the murli points in the Murli. Suggestions on what kind of thoughts etc. you could create are also given along with the explanations.

Contemplating on the BK knowledge is done through thinking about the knowledge, or murli point, deeply. This is called churning the knowledge. Churning involves thinking about the knowledge, or murli point, from all angles, with faith, until you become saturated with the knowledge so as to get the benefit of the churning process.

Indians churn the milk to get ghee which is highly valued. Hence, in the Hindu *Churning of the Ocean* myth, through the churning of the Ocean of Milk, nectar and a lot of other valuables are portrayed as being received. This reflects how through churning the BK knowledge, you get multimillion-fold benefits which are valuable and are like nectar, for example:

1. you are in the presence of God. So you experience intoxicating bliss which tastes like nectar.

2. you are able to receive God's help, etc. through your link to God.

3. you claim your inheritance from God, i.e. you regain your perfect divine state and perfect divine world where you enjoy happiness, status, wealth etc.

4. you become spiritually powerful. On this account you enjoy stability, spiritual strength, happiness, peace, purity, bliss, etc. in this and future births. The bliss which you enjoy, through churning the knowledge, increases as you become spiritually powerful.

5. you will no longer be disturbed by the vices. Thus, you can easily enjoy the intoxicating, blissful stage.

6. you have a better understanding of the knowledge given by God.

Your thoughts will be accurate, and elevated, when you are contemplating on the murli points which were given by God in the Murlis. This accuracy in thoughts will bring you into a high spiritually powerful stage because accurate, elevated thoughts are powerful thoughts.

Have faith that what has been said in the Murlis is the truth. This will help you to create powerful thoughts. Doubts will weaken your thoughts.

Each murli point is filled with power; you should also consider them to be powerful so that you can easily attain a high spiritual stage. Contemplating on the murli points includes creating thoughts based on the murli points and remembering what God has said in the Murlis. Remembering is part of the thinking process because new thoughts are created when you remember something.

If you constantly contemplate on the murli points,

waste thoughts would not be able to occupy any space within your mind and your intellect would also not be touched by waste. Thus, you can attain and maintain a high spiritually powerful stage easily.

One or more murli points should be contemplated upon each day so as to attain an elevated stage and to understand the knowledge, given by God, further. Through constantly contemplating on the murli points, the way you think will change and this will help you, thereafter, when you are reflecting on the knowledge. With time, as you keep ruminating upon the knowledge, you will find it easier to instantly go into a meditative state with just a thought.

When musing on a particular murli point, you should go into the depths of it. For example, when you think about God, consider everything that has been taught in the Murlis about God and, at the same time, bring yourself before Him through visualisations. Visualization involves creating thoughts with images. When your visualisations are based on what has been said in the Murlis, you will have powerful visualisations that bring you before God/Baba. These visualisations should include seeing yourself as the soul.

When you are thinking about the knowledge in the Murlis, with faith that it is true and with the intention to become spiritually powerful, you are making spiritual efforts to transform yourself into the divine state.

In this book, the word 'Baba', which means Father, is sometimes used while referring to God since God is the Father of the human souls. Sometimes, "God/Baba" is used just to leave more **impressions** within you (the soul) that God is your Father/Baba. Impressions of what you read, think, see, hear etc. are left on the energies of the soul and these are stored in the memory bank of the soul so that they can be remembered. When there are more impressions relating to God, they help you to easily remember God.

In this book, the explanations that have been given under the earlier murli extracts are not repeated unless there is a need to repeat something for giving proper explanations. Only new murli points are explained in the later chapters. Explanations are also not given if the explanations are there in the murli extract itself. The murli extracts, in the later chapters, are sometimes longer because a lot of the murli points have already been explained in the earlier chapters; so the reader should be able to understand what is being said in these later murli extracts. Some of the murli points are being repeated again and again because your thinking process has to change through being constantly exposed to the new way of thinking. These repetitions should also be a reminder to you that your new elevated thinking process involves repeatedly thinking the same or similar elevated thoughts.

Apart from using the murli extracts, explanations and suggestions in this book, so as to make sure that your thoughts are elevated thoughts, you can also contemplate on the knowledge in the articles, books, 'thoughts', etc. that are uploaded at the Brahma Kumaris website (https://www.brahma-kumaris.com). You can also do a search at https://www.bkgoogle.com to get the links for various kinds of BK material. Hence, you have access to numerous murli points, 'thoughts', explanations etc. which can be used, during your daily thinking, to improve your thinking process.

Brahma Kumari Pari, who was introduced to Brahma Kumaris Raja Yoga in 1994, wrote all the explanations in all the chapters of this book. She has also written others books and articles based on the knowledge of the Brahma Kumaris; these can be accessed through http://www.gbk-books.com/home.html, etc.

This "How to Think" book was edited and developed further by the other members of the "Shiv Baba Service Initiative", a team which is dedicated in doing Godly service through the abovementioned Brahma Kumaris website etc.

In 2018, the BK who manages the team "Shiv Baba Service Initiative", the BK Google search engine and the abovementioned Brahma Kumaris website had requested Brahma Kumari Pari to write the book titled "How to Think" since God (Shiv Baba) has said that this book should be written. Therefore, Brahma Kumari Pari took the initiative to get this book written. She enjoyed writing this book because it has helped her to get closer to God and has improved her thinking process.

1 SOUL

Murli Extract (SM 19-11-2018):

"The body of a person is visible with these eyes but the soul can be seen with divine vision. People have different features, but souls are not different; all are the same. It is just that the part of every soul is different. Human beings are big or small whereas souls are not bigger or smaller; the size of souls is the same."

Churning:

In the above Murli, the 1st murli point is "The body of a person is visible with these eyes but the soul can be seen with divine vision". While contemplating on this murli point, you can reflect on how you are the soul and not the physical body. You can think about how the body can be seen since it is material, whereas the soul cannot be seen with the eyes because the soul is a metaphysical point of living white light. The soul can only be seen in visions, and not everyone can see visions as they can see everything in the physical world. You can also contemplate on how:

1. the soul uses the mind, intellect and sanskaras (memories/impressions) which are also invisible, and

2. one cannot see the manner in which the soul is using the mind, intellect and sanskaras; one can only experience the result of the soul using them. For instance, you will know that you have taken a decision but you cannot see how the mind, intellect and sanskaras were used to make the decision. Neither can anyone else see how you have taken the decision through using their physical eyes.

You can also ruminate on the fact that you can experience the virtues but nobody can see them. This is different from how everyone can see the way your body is being used during your daily activities.

The words "People have different features, but souls are not different; all are the same", in the above murli extract, is the 2nd murli point. While contemplating on this murli point, you can think about how each physical body has different features whereas each soul is just a point of light. One would just see many 'points of lights' when one has a vision of seeing many souls.

The words "It is just that the part of every soul is different" is another murli point. While you ponder on this murli point, you can think about how each person is living a different kind of life, performing different roles.

The last or 4th murli point, in the above murli extract, is "Human beings are big or small whereas souls are not bigger or smaller; the size of souls is the same". When contemplating on this murli point, you can think about how the bodies of people may vary in size whereas each soul is only a point of light. You can also compare how the huge bodies are so limited in nature whereas the point of light is so unlimited since its energies can vibrate to go anywhere in the Corporeal World. During the Confluence Age, the energies of the soul can also go beyond the Corporeal World to reach the Angelic World.

While picking a murli point to churn on for the day, you can pick one from any of the above 4 murli points. However, when you churn on it, you can think about:

1. everything that has been said in this chapter.

2. all the knowledge which God has given on the soul.

When you are thinking about the metaphysical nature of the soul and the different parts of each soul, you can also contemplate on:

1. the soul's role that is portrayed through the world tree, and

2. how the soul takes many births, during each Cycle of Time (hereafter referred to as 'cycle').

When you think about the various aspects of the murli point, you are churning the knowledge. This churning process helps to connect you to the Ocean of Knowledge (God/Baba) and you will be churning the Ocean of Knowledge to receive all the valuable benefits. Therefore, you should constantly think about the murli points so as to remain involved with the churning process.

2 ORIGINAL AND ETERNAL FORM

Murli extract (AM 13-3-2016):

"Your original form was not that of impurity. Both your eternal and your original forms are pure. Impurity is artificial; it is not real. ...Simply have this one thought: Originally and eternally, my real form is of a pure soul. Whenever you see others, look at their original and eternal real forms. Look at these forms of yourself and of others and realise the real form!"

Churning:

The original qualities of the soul are the virtues and powers. This means that the soul was originally only filled with pure energies. The vices (impurities) are not our original qualities. The pure ordinary energies of the soul transform into the impure state when we yield to the vices. As a result, the vices exist within the soul. These impure energies (vices) are not the original form, or part of the original form, of the soul. The soul's original form, eternally, is only the pure form. Due to the weak ordinary state, the vices have made us think that we are also the impure energies. You should stop thinking in this way because what you think affects the state which you are in. If you keep thinking that you are the pure virtuous soul, you easily attain the pure virtuous state, i.e. you will enjoy being your pure virtuous self. See yourself as the soul seated on your seat in the center of the forehead because this will help you to enjoy the highest spiritual stage. Since this thought is created based on the BK knowledge, it initiates the link to God; so you attain this pure elevated stage.

When you see yourself as the soul, you are creating thoughts to this effect. When you (the soul) create such a thought in your mind, an impression of the thought is left on the pure energies of the soul because you have been brought into the pure state when the thought is created. Your intellect, then, takes the impression of the thought into the memory bank of the soul. Since the impression is left on pure energies and these energies remain in the pure state, within the memory bank, they help you to remain pure; the purity within the soul increases as you keep accumulating these pure thoughts within the soul. Thus, keep creating numerous thoughts to the effect that you are the pure virtuous soul. It helps you to experience your original, eternal, true form. When you are in this stage, you know that this is your real form.

When your spiritual stage is bad, negative or waste thoughts can get created in your mind and these also get stored in your memory bank. The energies, which these impressions are left on, become impure since:

1. the impressions are left on weak ordinary energies, and

2. they are exposed to impurities.

Hence, impure energies accumulate within the soul when you keep entertaining negative/waste thoughts. As a consequence, you get spiritually weaker. So do not indulge in thinking negative/waste thoughts. They will also make you think that the vices are a part of you. Keep remembering that the vices are not a part of the real you.

When you see others as the soul seated on their seat in the center of their forehead, it will help them to remain in the pure virtuous state too. When they are in the pure state, they will be very co-operative. So they will easily flow along with what you are doing and they will not give you a difficult time. Therefore, constantly have the thought that they are the pure souls who are seated on their seat in the center of their forehead, and keep seeing them as souls when you talk to them. This will help you to realise that their real form is also the pure form.

3   GOD IS A POINT

Murli Extract (SM 19-11-2018):

"So, God is extremely subtle. There isn't anything as subtle as He is. He is an absolutely tiny point. It is because He is so subtle that no one knows Him. Although the sky is also said to be subtle, it is called space. There are the five elements. He comes and enters a body of the five elements. He is so subtle. He is an absolutely tiny point."

Churning:

Though God is an Ocean of Virtues and Powers, He is just a Point of Light. Since he is just a point, it is difficult to see Him. Further, God's energies are metaphysical;

hence God is 'so subtle' and not capable of being seen by the eyes. For all these reasons, people do not know anything about God. They also do not know Him if they do not have a link to Him.

People can see what is in the Corporeal World because the energies of the Corporeal World occupy a huge space and the energies of the Corporeal World are not metaphysical. What exists in the Corporeal World consists of denser energies and material stuff. These can be seen or detected. Therefore, people know that the physical world and physical body exists, and they know quite a lot about these.

The murli points, in the above murli extract, can be contemplated on while remembering God. Through doing this, you know Him. When you remember God/Baba, you could visualise an image of Him as a point or as an enlarged point. You visualize through creating thoughts with images in your mind. Create the image of God with the thought that you are in His Company and you will be with God through your link to Him.

Whenever you remember God, a new thought is created and this new thought leaves a new impression on the energies of the soul. These energies of the soul become pure powerful energies since pure powerful impressions of God have been left on them. When you keep remembering God, more and more of such powerful impressions are left within the soul; hence you acquire the ability to easily connect yourself to God. As a consequence, you can easily become spiritually powerful and pure through absorbing powerful energies from God via your link to God. The purity of the soul increases as your energies keep transforming into the pure state. You become more powerful due to this and due to the presence of God's powerful energies within you (the soul).

When churning on a murli point about God, you can think of His divine attributes, acts and all the knowledge which has been given about God in the BK Murlis. You should also think about how God has come to recreate your divine world by establishing the Confluence Age. When thinking about God, always keep in mind that He is a Point of Light. Think of how fortunate you are to have finally met God Himself through your power of yoga and through His corporeal chariots.

4   FATHER TEACHES SOULS

Murli Extract (SM 13-2-2018):

"The Father says: I am once again teaching you Raja
Yoga. ...He sits here and speaks to you souls. There isn't
a scholar etc. who would sit and speak to souls in this
way and say that he is their father. You souls are
incorporeal. I too am incorporeal."

Churning:

When incorporeal God speaks the Murli to the crowd,
which is in front of Him, He is actually speaking to the
incorporeal souls. This helps the souls to attain the
blissful soul conscious stage. Even when we hear the
Murli, or read the Murli, with the view that the words

are from God, God is still speaking to the souls through those words because the words, in the Murlis, were intended for the souls. Therefore, the souls will hear God's Sounds of Silence through those words too, as the souls use their physical bodies to hear/read the words of the Murli. This is so because God is also speaking those words to the souls in the subtle region (Angelic World) as they hear/read them.

When I was hearing the Sakar Murli in the early morning hours, in the BK center, I knew that God was also speaking the Sakar Murli to me in the subtle region as the BK (a member of the Brahma Kumaris) was reading the Murli. Sometimes:

1. I would see myself in the subtle region and God would be subtly speaking those same words to me as I was also listening to them through the physical body. Though I was in the Angelic World, I knew that I was also hearing it through the body which was in the Corporeal World that was far below the Angelic World.

2. I would experience myself as Parvati (in the subtle region) listening to what God Shiva was saying. I would not be aware that I was also listening to the words through the physical body, I would only be listening to it in the subtle region. It was only when I begin to drop back into the physical body that I would be aware that the BK was also reading the same words as that which I was hearing in the subtle region.

3. I would in the body listening to the Murli but I can also hear it in the subtle region at the same time. I would be aware that I am in both worlds (Angelic World and Corporeal World).

4. I would only be listening to the Murli in the Corporeal World, even though my spiritual stage is quite high. I would experience the blissful stage while using the body to listen to the Murli. Though I am only listening to the words in the Corporeal World, I know that I am linked to God through hearing the Murli; I know that I am becoming spiritually powerful through hearing and accepting those words. Actually, I noticed this from the first time when I was hearing the Sakar Murli in the BK center. No one told me that this would happen. I wanted to listen to the sakar murli because I wanted to become a serious intense spiritual effort maker. Then, while listening to the sakar murli, I noticed that it was helping me to attain a very high spiritual stage; I would experience intoxicating bliss. So I would always concentrate on **only hearing the Murli** and would not think of anything else at that time.

If my attention is turned away from the words in the murli, vices could emerge. When they emerge, I am completely in the body and my spiritual stage is not high. I will also not hear God speaking those subtle words because God is speaking those same words to us in the subtle region. We are only in the subtle region when our spiritual stage is high. So I have to attain a higher stage to become aware that God is subtly speaking those same words to me as I am listening to them through the physical body. What we hear in the subtle region is God's powerful Sounds of Silence.

Many BKs might not be aware that they are also listening to the Murli in the subtle region because they do not have developed psychic abilities as I have. God's Sounds of Silence will always accompany the words that have been spoken by Him through the Murlis; thus, God is speaking to you (the soul). Keep reading, or listening to, the Murlis with the thought that you are also **subtly listening to what God is saying in the subtle region**. It will help you to easily attain a high spiritual stage.

From 1994, I knew that God was guiding me to practice Brahma Kumaris Raja Yoga and to accept that I was a deity soul. From 1996, I often experienced God as my Father. I knew that God, my Father, was helping and guiding me.

God teaches the souls Raja Yoga through the Murlis which are given in the Brahma Kumaris, i.e. God teaches us to have yoga with Him through our thoughts. This yoga is the highest kind of yoga and we can only have yoga with incorporeal God at the end of the cycle through using the knowledge given by God in the BK Murlis. Through this yoga, we receive God's energies, and so we (the souls) are empowered to sit on our seat in the center of the forehead. Through being empowered, we also transform into the divine state; this is also one of the main aims why God began teaching us Raja Yoga. To practice Raja Yoga, all the thoughts which we create must be based on what God has taught us in the Murlis.

Murli Extract (SM 18-10-18):

"The spiritual Father explains to you spiritual children what a soul is and who the Supreme Soul, his Father, is. He explains this once again because this is an impure world. Those who are impure are always senseless. ...The soul remembers his Supreme Father, the Supreme Soul. It is a physical father who gives birth to this body whereas that Supreme Father, the Supreme Soul, is the parlokik Father, the Father of souls. ...God, the Father, would definitely be the incorporeal One. ...You understand that you souls shed bodies and take others. ...You have the faith: I am a soul and this is my body. The body is perishable whereas the imperishable soul is a child of that Supreme Father, the Supreme Soul. ...It is the soul that takes many births. His father changes in every birth. ...No one, apart from the unlimited Father, can grant souls a vision of God. ...You have two fathers: one is a perishable father who gives birth to a perishable body. The other is the imperishable Father of imperishable souls. ...The Father comes here and teaches you souls. Souls listen through their physical senses. The soul has received these eyes with which to see and ears with which to hear."

Churning:

Shiv Baba is our parlokik Father. Parlokik Father mean 'Father from beyond' or 'spiritual Father'. God is the imperishable spiritual Father of the imperishable souls. God keeps repeating the knowledge, about the soul and Supreme Soul, to us because:

1. we (the souls) were in an impure state living in an impure world; thus, we had firmly formed the view that we were the bodies and that the father of the physical body is our father.

2. we had forgotten that we are the souls and we will find it very difficult to accept that we are the souls when we are in the body-conscious state.

3. we had begun to belief all sorts of things about God, during the second half cycle, when we were not aware of who God is.

4. we have to experience the truth in a practical way, through our attention constantly being turned towards the truth and through our minds being filled with the truth.

5. the 'way we think' has to be changed.

We have to change the way we think so as to have firm

faith that we are the souls and not the bodies, and that God (the Supreme Soul) is our spiritual Father. To stand firm in your faith, you have to:

1. keep listening to, or keep reading, the Murlis where Baba keeps repeating this, and

2. keep creating thoughts to this effect.

Though we can accept it that God is our Father when we hear it, we have to keep creating thoughts to this effect so as to make sure that all the old teachings no longer have an influence over us. This involves taking the initiative to change the way we think.

5   SOUL CONSCIOUSNESS

Murli Extract (SM 22-12-2018):

"Baba says: Become soul conscious, that is, consider
yourself to be bodiless."

Churning:

When you see yourself as the soul and not as the body,
you (the soul) get detached from your body and you will
feel that you are the soul in the body. This is the soul
conscious stage, i.e. it is the bodiless or incorporeal
stage. You will be seated on your seat in the centre of
the forehead when you are soul conscious.

When non-BKs see themselves as the soul, they do not
go into the high soul conscious stage. They may just get

detached to go into the state of being the soul. As a soul, in a detached state, they can become inundated with the vices.

When we see ourselves as the soul, we become soul conscious because we are linked to God. This soul conscious stage is the stage which we will be in when we are in the Golden Age. To easily attain the soul conscious stage, you can do the following:

1. Remember that Baba has told you to become soul conscious (through seeing yourself as the soul).

2. Remember that you are the soul and also remember Baba.

3. See yourself as the soul seated on your seat in the centre of the forehead. When you do this, you will actually be positioned on that seat because you are getting God's assistance to do this.

4. Remember that you are linked to God as you see yourself as the soul.

To attain and remain in the soul conscious stage, you have to see yourself as the soul and/or remember God **with faith** that you are a soul and that God is the Supreme Soul. Through becoming soul conscious, you will see or know that God is guiding you; you will hear God speaking to you because God is **subtly communicating with the soul**.

6 REMEMBER THE FATHER

Murli Extract (SM 13-2-2018):

"Constantly remember Me alone. Connect your
intellects in yoga to Me up above."

Churning:

Remembering is actually part of our thinking process.
While you remember God/Baba, your intellect is
bringing earlier thoughts etc. (which are stored as
memories in your memory bank) into your mind and
another similar thought is created. Even when you
remember the knowledge that has been given by Baba,
you are remembering Baba.

When you keep remembering God/Baba, you are

creating more and more similar thoughts. All these similar thoughts are like a thought within your memory bank. Each subsequent thought will be energising the earlier thought that exists within the memory bank. As they energise the earlier thought, a more powerful memory exists in the memory bank and this more powerful memory is emerged by the intellect when you remember Baba subsequently. The powerful memory combines with your current thought to create a very powerful thought; so you can easily get linked to God.

The similar thoughts which keep getting accumulated in the memory bank will also be influencing you from the memory bank. They influence how you think and act because they have become powerful. The intellect will keep bringing these influential memories into the mind since you have the desire to keep remembering them and since they are influential. The intellect will be empowered as it brings these memories into the mind since the intellect will constantly be exposed to the pure energies which have the impressions of pure elevated thoughts. This and remembering Baba (or remembering the knowledge given by Baba), together, will empower your intellect and so it will fly to the Angelic World. Hence, you get connected to God who is in the Angelic World, i.e. you are in yoga with God/Baba. As a consequence, you become spiritually empowered by the energies of God which flow into you through your link to God.

When you keep remembering Baba, the memory will

become so powerful that it plays the greatest influencing role from your memory bank; hence, you will be constantly influenced to remember Baba and think about the knowledge which He has given. Since it influences the way you think, remembering God/Baba is a very effective way of changing the way you think. Since powerful memories will easily influence you, create powerful memories through having faith in Baba and the knowledge which He has given.

When you remember Baba, you could also create another new different thought based on what you have remembered, e.g. you could create a new thought that Baba is the Ocean of Love and that He is showering you with love etc. All these will also influence you from the memory bank since they will become part of the group of memories which are used when remembering Baba. Creating new different thoughts can be entertaining; so you will not seek entertainment elsewhere and you will enjoy your spiritual life through easy spiritual effort making. Further, love helps to easily link you to God and it will also help you to remain linked to God. So keep absorbing love from God. Keep visualising that God's vibrations of love are constantly flowing into you.

Spiritual life can be blissful when you have your link to God. Thus, keep remembering Baba to have a strong link to God. The stronger your link, the greater your bond with God.

7 CLOSE RELATIONSHIP WITH ONLY ONE GOD

Murli Extract (SM 19-7-2018):

"The Father now says: Break away from everyone else and connect yourself to Me alone: mine is one Shiv Baba and none other. You are the Mother and Father."

Churning:

In the above murli extract, Baba informs that we should only have a close relationship with Him. This will help us to easily establish our link to God so as to become spiritually powerful. We should constantly be creating thoughts to the effect "mine is one Shiv Baba and none other" or "Baba, you are my Mother and Father". You can also enjoy other relationships with God, for example, you can see God as your Teacher, Satguru, Companion, Child, Husband, Wife, Friend, etc. If you do not have a close relationship with God, you will find it difficult to become spiritually powerful, and you can easily be consumed by the vices. Consequently, you will experience unhappiness, dissatisfaction etc. and will be troubled by waste/negative thoughts.

No benefits are received through remembering others whereas you get a multimillion-fold benefit, through the Law of Karma, for remembering Baba. In fact, remembering others will only create further karmic accounts.

Having attachment to others will also prevent you from remembering Baba because you will be remembering others. Hence, you will find it more difficult to attain a powerful spiritual stage.

You are, actually, yielding to the vices if you have attachment for others. For this reason too, you will find it difficult to establish a strong link to God.

You might also be influenced by the ordinary impure vibrations which are being emitted from others if you have attachment for them. When you are exposed to impure vibrations from others, you will struggle harder to establish a strong link to God.

If you only remember Baba, you get connected to the Powerhouse (God); so you get filled His Love, Purity,

Power, Happiness, Peace, Bliss and the Knowledge which exists within Him. These will get downloaded into you through your intellect and mind, when you are linked to God. You (the soul) will also become like Him since you will be radiating His energies. God's energies, which radiate from you, will make others peaceful & happy too.

To keep others happy and contented, make sure that they constantly get soaked with Baba's love which vibrates out from you. Keep your spiritual stage high so that they can get this benefit through you. Change the way you think so that you constantly see others with pure love, for example:

1. think about how the other human souls are living in the impure Kaliyug world. When they are deprived of love, they would feel angry, lonely, etc.

2. think about how fortunate you are that you are able to receive love directly from God.

3. think about how the others are not able to receive love directly from God, due to their weak state. Remind yourself that you should keep the others happy and contented through sending them God's love because they want to be loved and are not able to receive love directly from God.

4. remember that all souls are the children of God and that we all belong to the same *world family*. Hence, we should be helping each other.

5. if the others are your lokik family members, remember that you have a duty to keep them happy. So keep remembering Baba so that you can constantly receive God's love etc. and send it to them.

6. remember that God has come to help all His children (all human souls). Consider yourself to be an instrument of God. As an instrument of God, absorb God's energies and send it to others.

8 PURIFICATION THROUGH REMEMBRANCE

Murli Extract (SM 22-11-2016):

"The Father says: Live at home with your family and simply remember Baba. That's all! Baba alone is the Purifier. The Father says: Remember Me and I guarantee that all your sins will be absolved. ...Make yourself egoless and free from attachment. No one can benefit without having remembrance of Baba. The more you remember Him, the purer you will become."

Churning:

Only Baba/God is the Purifier and it is only when you remember Baba/God that you get purified; your sins will get burnt away and your energies will get transformed into pure divine state. The more you remember God, the purer you become. Hence, keep creating thoughts about the knowledge which He has given and keep remembering Him.

Do not have attachment to anything or anyone else. Make sure that there is no attachment to:

1. your impure ideas, opinions, beliefs, memories, etc.

2. your job, possessions, etc.

3. other human beings.

4. your physical body.

Constantly sending God's love to others will keep them in a pure state. Thus, they will be cooperative. Your family members will also not mind your spiritual efforts to remain pure and remember only Baba. When you keep sending them God's energies, they will be contented; so they will not expect you to act in an impure way. When you are sending them God's vibrations, you are also remembering Baba; so you become purer.

You have to take care of your body with pure love since even the quantum and other cosmic energies, which provide the body, want to be exposed to purity and pure love. However, you should not have attachment to the body because this will prevent you from going beyond the physical body to attain a high spiritual stage.

Having ego or attachment will prevent you from going into the bodiless stage (soul conscious stage). Therefore, make sure that you do not have ego and attachment through keeping a watch on your thoughts.

9   IMBIBE

Murli Extract (SM 20-11-2018):

"Those who do not become soul conscious cannot imbibe this knowledge."

Churning:

To imbibe/absorb knowledge, you have to contemplate on a murli point or listen to (or read) a Murli. Reading, listening to and contemplating on the murli points should be enjoyed and there should be acceptance of the knowledge.

If you were contemplating on the murli point that you are a 'soul who has taken many births through the cycle', the first stage of the churning process is that you should believe that you are a soul (a point of light) and that time does flow in a cyclic manner. In addition to this, you have to imbibe or absorb the murli point. This means that you have to constantly see yourself as the soul who has taken many births and is now in the Confluence Age with God; you have to create numerous thoughts to this effect. Have the feeling that you are the soul experiencing the soul conscious stage. Sustain this feeling by soaking yourself up with numerous thoughts to this effect. Create powerful thoughts, through having faith, so that your mind and intellect are filled with these powerful thoughts. Create these powerful thoughts as you read and contemplate on the words in the Murli. When you do this, your mind and intellect gets filled with powerful thoughts. Your mind will be filled with the powerful thoughts that you create and with the information which have been brought by the intellect into the mind (based on your thoughts). The information which the intellect brings from the memory bank includes:

1. the BK knowledge which you received before this.

2. the thoughts that you previously created, based on the BK knowledge.

3. your experiences based on the BK knowledge.

The intellect gets filled with powerful thoughts:

1. as you use it to churn the knowledge, and

2. as the intellect takes powerful thoughts etc. to and fro between the memory bank and the mind.

The mind and intellect getting filled with powerful thoughts etc. are all part of the stage of absorption. Since your mind and intellect is filled with pure positive thoughts and knowledge, waste/negative thoughts cannot come near. The vices remain distant because you are getting filled with God's energies and are becoming spiritually powerful. The initial stage of absorption then goes into the final stage of absorption where you experience yourself as the blissful soul. As you absorb/imbibe the knowledge, you become soul conscious.

You can become soul conscious through remembering any murli point that has been given by God in the Murlis. As you become soul conscious, you imbibe what you are contemplating on; as a consequence, you have a relevant experience.

Murli Extract (AM 26-11-1979):

"Imbibe Baba's virtues and become the Master of all His qualities."

Churning:

As you imbibe the knowledge and become soul
conscious, you get linked to God and God's vibrations
will flow into you. Hence, you will also be
imbibing/absorbing God's Virtues and Powers. As you
imbibe Baba's Virtues and Powers, you become a
Master of all His qualities. Therefore, keep churning the
BK knowledge so as to enjoy this final stage, through
which you become spiritually powerful.

10   ORIGINAL RELIGION

Murli Extract (SM 23-7-2018):

"Baba has explained that you do not have to go anywhere for peace. You have to continue to perform actions. You have to practise being bodiless: I am a soul and these are my organs. The original religion of souls is peace."

Churning:

Peace is the original religion of the soul. This is so because the original qualities of the soul are only the virtues and powers. When one is only filled with all the virtues and powers, one is peaceful. No vice will exist within you when you are in the original peaceful state.

One is stable in the original religion of the soul when one is soul conscious. When one is stabilised in the original religion of the soul, one will naturally behave in a virtuous, peaceful manner.

During the first half cycle, since the people were constantly soul conscious, they were only under the influence of the original religion of the soul; so they were living a virtuous, peaceful life. When one has a virtuous lifestyle, due to constantly remaining stable in the original religion of the soul, one is putting the original religion of the soul into practice. It is **only** during the first half cycle that souls constantly remain soul conscious and so they constantly remain stable in the original religion of the soul; it is **only** the people of the first half cycle who put the original religion of the soul into practice. This was why their world was peaceful. Since the people of the second half cycle are in the weaker ordinary state, they are not soul conscious and they are capable of being overwhelmed by the vices. Hence, the people in the second half cycle are not living in a peaceful world; they are not capable of putting the original religion of the soul into practice.

The human souls no longer had the ability to remain soul conscious, when the deities lost their divine state at the end of the Silver Age. Since the people were capable of getting inundated with the vices, spiritual and yogic practices were created so as to make sure that the people continued to live a peaceful, virtuous life-style. These practices became part of the Hindu religion that continued in place of the Original Eternal Deity Religion (Adi Sanatan Devi Devta Dharam). Thus, the emphasis in Hinduism is in respect of how the life is lived and this is why it is said that the Hindu religion is a way of living.

The Hindu religion is the changed/mutated form of the Adi Sanatan Devi Devta Dharam. The people of the Adi Sanatan Devi Devta Dharam practiced the original religion of the soul. The pure, divine, peaceful, virtuous way of life lived by the deities during the Golden and Silver Ages is the Adi Sanatan Devi-Devta Dharma. God established the Adi Sanatan Devi Devta Dharma through the Confluence Age. Adi means 'the first', 'from the beginning' or 'the original'. Sanatan means 'ancient, eternal and beyond the dimension of time'. Dharma means 'religion' and 'way of life of the soul'. Devi Devta means 'deities'.

From the beginning of the Copper Age, religions and codes of conduct were created to keep people on the virtuous, peaceful path. These religions included worship to God so that the people could turn to God for help when life is unbearable, painful, etc. The human beings, who lived during the first half cycle, did not practice any religion (like how the people of the second half cycle do) because:

1. they got everything they wanted since they were constantly soul conscious. They did not have to worship God to ask Him for anything. It is only the people of the

second half cycle who ask God for something or the other; they do not get everything they want due to the weaker state and the settling process.

2. they were naturally pure, virtuous, happy and contented due to constantly remaining soul conscious. The vices did not exist to trouble them and so they were naturally putting the original religion of the soul into practice. It is only the people of the second half cycle who are troubled by the vices; hence they have to turn to God for help.

Now, during the Confluence Age, through the elevated thinking process, we become soul conscious. As a result, we experience peace (the original religion of the soul), and this influences us to conduct ourselves in a virtuous angelic manner. We do not have to follow any code of conduct that has been established for religions because, when we are soul conscious, we will automatically be living a virtuous lifestyle. Through just remembering Baba and the knowledge which He has given, we become soul conscious; so we remain stable in the original religion of the soul. As spiritual effort makers, we should make spiritual efforts to remain stable in the original religion of the soul while performing our daily activities. No matter what kind of situation you are in, you would be able to remain peaceful so long as you are soul conscious. You do not have to go anywhere to enjoy peace. You can enjoy the original peaceful state through remaining in the bodiless, soul conscious stage.

Constantly remain stable in the original religion of the soul through seeing yourself as the soul seated on its seat at the centre of the forehead. The more you see yourself as the soul, an embodiment of peace, the higher the spiritual stage you attain and the greater you are stabilised in the original religion of the soul.

As you keep remembering that you are the soul, you absorb/imbibe the knowledge that you are the soul; so you (the soul), along with your intellect, get empowered by the words in the knowledge (through God's Sounds of Silence which accompany the words in the knowledge). Consequently, you experience the final stage of absorption through which you become stable in the original religion of the soul.

Based on my experiences, I will say that life is very good and peaceful when we are stable in the original religion of the soul. No matter what is happening around me, I am able to remain peaceful **when I am making spiritual efforts** to remember Baba. I remain peaceful because I have been stabilised in the original religion of the soul through my spiritual effort making. You can also have a peaceful and blissful life through using this elevated thinking process.

11   EMBODIMENT

Murli Extract (AM 17-2-2019):

"When milk is churned for butter, there is first a lot of expansion (quantity), and then the butter is extracted from the essence. ...Become an embodiment of the essence and make others that."

Churning:

The word 'expansion' involves using the physical body. When you are involved with thinking thoughts at the grosser level, you are involved with expansion because you use the physical body to create the thoughts in the mind.

Often, BKs begin contemplating on the BK knowledge

when their spiritual stage is weak. Thus, they have to create numerous thoughts, based on the BK knowledge, to attain the bodiless stage. They use their body to create these thoughts; for this reason and since their spiritual stage is bad, they are greatly involved with 'expansion'. However, their thoughts are elevated thoughts while they are churning, and these elevated thoughts bring them into the stage of being an embodiment of the essence.

If your spiritual stage was already high, you need not create so many thoughts to become an embodiment. Just one thought will bring you into the stage of being the embodiment because you will be creating a powerful thought. However, initially, beginners will be creating numerous thoughts to attain a high stage. Then, just a powerful thought will bring them into the stage of being an embodiment of the essence.

In the body-conscious state, we think that we are the body and this is an expansion of the body. We are no longer aware that we are the souls while we are in the body-conscious state. You have to change this through your thoughts so that you go from expansion to the essence (soul); as a consequence of which you will feel that you are the soul and not the body.

When we are body-conscious, we can think waste/negative thoughts; thinking waste/negative thoughts is also an 'expansion' of the physical body. The vices (including the ability to think negative/waste thoughts) came into existence when we became body-conscious at the beginning of the Copper Age. Now, through remembrance of God and His knowledge, you can become an embodiment of the essence despite all the attempts by the vices to keep you in the body-conscious state. When you become a powerful spiritual effort maker, the vices will try their best to remain in control, but you can be victorious through remembering Baba.

Often, when we begin making spiritual efforts, we have the feeling that we are **in** the physical body. When we experience the soul conscious stage, we would **not** experience being **in** the body. The **soul conscious stage** is the stage where one is an **embodiment of the essence**. Normally, we are only soul conscious for a split second and then, we slowly lose that stage to come back into the body. If we continued to make spiritual efforts we can bring our intellect and consciousness into the Angelic World again, instead of keeping them within the body; we are actually making spiritual efforts to go from expansion to the essence. From all that which has been said in this paragraph, it can be said that there is a lot of expansion before the butter (representing that which tastes very good and is beneficial) is extracted from the essence.

Butter being extracted from the essence also includes how the divine virtues and powers, which are deeper down within the soul, are emerged as we churn the knowledge. These divine virtues and powers sank deeper down when we lost our divine state at the end of the Silver Age. Now, they emerge again when we remember that we are the deity souls who are being empowered by God to transform into the deities again. Hence, the butter (divine virtues and powers) is extracted from the essence (soul). Before these divine virtues and powers emerged, we were filled with the weak ordinary energies and so we were indulging in the vices, i.e. we were involved with expansion. This ordinary state no longer exists when the divine virtues and powers emerge from deeper within. As soon as the divine virtues and powers emerge from deeper within, you become soul conscious because the 'divine virtues and powers emerging from deeper within' is **part of the process** which enables you to enjoy a stronger link to God.

The deity souls have an inherent ability to transform back into the divine state; hence, through exposure to God's energies, the deity souls transform. This transformation process also involves extracting the butter (divine state) due to the inherent ability of the deity soul. We also have this inherent ability because the divine virtues and powers exist deeper down within the soul and they are emerged during the transformation process.

You can emerge the divine virtues and powers, from deeper within, through the thought that you are emerging them. These divine virtues and powers will also automatically be emerging from deeper within, as you keep churning the knowledge.

When you are contemplating on the knowledge, you are churning. Through this churning process, you will be able to extract the butter from the milk. The milk is the 'knowledge given by God along with God's energies which accompany the knowledge'. Since you are exposed to God's energies that accompany the knowledge, your week ordinary energies are transformed into the divine state. You are also extracting butter through this.

When we churn the knowledge, we are extracting butter through this churning process **as we attain the stage of being an embodiment of the essence**. The 'stage of being an embodiment of the essence' itself is also butter that has been extracted. This butter is extracted through the soul getting filled with God's Virtues and Powers, i.e. we are getting filled from the Essence (Supreme Soul). We extract the butter when the **Essence (God) and the essence (the deity soul)** are in the combined form through yoga.

When we absorb from the Essence (Supreme Soul) through the churning process, we experience bliss. The blissful stage is also butter that has been extracted through what is received from the Essence (God). You will only experience bliss as you attain the soul conscious stage. Hence, to extract the butter, one has to become soul conscious (an embodiment of the essence).

When you are in a high stage, you will also have a better understanding of the knowledge that has been given by God; this benefit is also 'butter' that gets extracted through the churning process. The better understanding of the knowledge will help you to easily become an embodiment of the essence.

To become an embodiment of the essence, you have to keep remembering:

1. God.

2. that you are a soul.

3. the knowledge given by God in the Murlis.

4. your experiences and further understanding on the knowledge.

Through this remembrance you experience the final stage of absorption which enables you to experience the stage of being an embodiment. This is also the final stage of the churning process. While in this stage, you will experience yourself as the pure, imperishable soul who is the child of God, and you will know that you are not the perishable body; you have gone from expansion to the essence.

BKs carry out actions with the body while creating elevated thoughts to attain the soul conscious stage, that is, they perform karma yoga. Therefore, they are involved with 'expansion' (since they are performing actions with the body) while making spiritual efforts to become an embodiment of the essence. Since their thoughts are elevated thoughts that are based on the BK knowledge, they can easily become soul conscious while carrying out actions through using the body.

For the sake of world transformation, we have to make sure that we assist others to become an embodiment of the essence. This involves doing service; we have to do service while making spiritual efforts to become, and remain, an embodiment of the essence. While doing service, it is very easy to go into the expansion (body-consciousness); so we have to be extra careful to keep a check on our thoughts, feelings, actions, words, etc. When we see ourselves going into expansion, we have to keep remembering Baba so that we get His assistance to become, and remain, an embodiment of the essence.

You have to use the body, i.e. go into expansion, so as to make spiritual efforts and do service. This means that you have to use the body to become spiritually powerful and receive a multimillion-fold benefit through the Law of Karma. So use the body, as much as you can, for your own benefit.

12 RECOGNIZING AND KNOWING GOD

Murli Extract (SM 16-11-2018):

"By recognizing the Father, human beings become like diamonds. By not knowing Him, human beings become like shells and completely impure. By knowing the Father, they become pure. There is no one pure in the impure world."

Churning:

The **state of the human soul and the life it lives** are valuable during the Confluence Age and are worthless in the Kaliyug world. Since a diamond is considered to be very valuable in the current world, Baba compares our Confluence Aged state to that of a diamond. In contrast, Baba says that the Kaliyug state is like a shell since a shell is considered to be worthless in the present world. It should be noted that the state of the soul is reflected through the human beings, i.e. through their personality, behaviour etc.

In the second half cycle, it is as if the souls and human beings become hollow like a shell because:

1. the spiritual light of the souls gets reduced (until it is almost extinguishing by the end of the cycle).

2. souls, and human beings, no longer have divine qualities.

3. people do not have good values when they are overcome by the vices.

In the second half cycle, the souls also look ordinary with no glow, like the shell, since the souls are in the ordinary state. Due to this weak ordinary state, the souls become impure. The state of the human souls, human beings and the lives that are lived are worthless, in the Kaliyug world, because:

1. the people/souls in the Kaliyug world are only becoming more impure and so the world which they live in becomes more impure.

2. the people in the Kaliyug world cannot recognise God since they do not have the knowledge which God has

given through the Murli, and they do not have a direct link to God.

3. the people experience sorrow in the Kaliyug world (since they are in the impure state and are living in an impure world).

4. the people are living in 'hell' on earth. This is also a reason why people die more quickly and why deities cannot be born in the second half cycle.

The Kaliyug world is an ordinary, imperfect, valueless, impure world; this world is transformed into the divine, perfect, valuable, pure world when we become like diamonds through recognizing and knowing the Father/God during the Confluence Age. The state of the human soul and the life it lives is valuable, during the Confluence Age, because:

1. we bring benefit to the world through the transformation process.

2. we enjoy bliss through being linked to God.

3. we enjoy great benefits, through the Law of Karma, when we make spiritual efforts to shine brilliantly like a diamond.

4. it is only during the Confluence Age that we can be close to God through having a direct link to Him. We cannot do this at any other time in the cycle.

It is only during the Confluence Age that we see and

recognise the Father, since we have been given a link to him. Due to this recognition, we make intense spiritual efforts to regain our perfect, divine state and world. As a consequence, we transform to become diamonds and the world also transforms into the pure divine state.

After the soul has recognised the Father, the soul will continue to know that it is with God through the link to God. It knows that it is getting linked to God through using the knowledge; this will influence the person to value the knowledge.

During the Confluence Age, we know a lot about God because God has given this knowledge to us. By virtue of contemplating on the knowledge, we get linked to God; so we get to know Him better in a practical way. Through knowing God in this way, the soul within the human being would be looking brilliant, like a diamond, since the soul is filled with God's energies, purity, etc. The state, which the soul is in, is reflected through the human being; therefore, the conduct of the person would be sweet and angelic. Through this angelic state and life, the whole world is transformed into the pure divine perfect state.

During the first half cycle, though we are not filled with knowledge and God's energies, we (the souls) would also be looking brilliant since the souls are in the divine state filled with purity, divine virtues and powers. This gets reflected through the divine conduct of the deities; they would be like pure diamonds without any defect.

Since it is a pure world, it would be heaven on earth. These human beings would enjoy living a heavenly life because the world is transformed through the Confluence Age. It is being transformed now since we recognise and know God.

You will surely recognise the Father when you are in the stage of being an embodiment. Since you are with the Father, you will be filled with God's energies, and you get purified; thus you will be shining brilliantly like a diamond. You will be valuable to the whole world and will be living a valuable life since you are involved with world transformation. Then, you take births in the first half cycle and will be like a jewel there too, due to having become pure through the Confluence Age.

When I was hearing the Sakar Murli, for the first time and thereafter, during the early morning hours, in the BK center, there was an instant recognition of God as soon as I became soul conscious. I knew that there was only one God and that this was the same God:

1. who was guiding me before I came into the Brahma Kumaris.

2. who spoke the Sakar Murli through Brahma Baba when Brahma Baba was in the sakar form.

Before I was introduced to the Brahma Kumaris, I knew that God was guiding me but I could not see Him. I did not know anything about Him. From my experiences, I knew that He was not in the world which I was living in.

I knew that He was helping me from a higher dimension which was beyond the sky. However, I did not know where that dimension was. When I needed something, He would bring it before me; somehow I will be getting it. I did not have to make any efforts to get it. These things are those which are helping me now to do service etc. For instance, since I was a trained music teacher before I became a lawyer, I know how to teach spiritual knowledge to others now. The fact that I began developing my power of concentration and the ability to easily go within (through meditating), before I was introduced to the BK gyan/knowledge, helped me to instantly know that there is something really brilliant going on within the Brahma Kumaris when I was introduced to the Brahma Kumaris. These powerful impressions have helped me, until now, to:

1. remain an intense spiritual effort maker,

2. continue doing Godly service through using my specialities.

Now, based on experiences, I know who God is and, when I am in the subtle region, I know that I am with God there. I never had such feelings before I was introduced to the Brahma Kumaris. Before I became a member of the Brahma Kumaris, I was wondering about who God was and from where He was helping me. From my experiences, before I was introduced to the BK knowledge, I knew that God was not the energies of the Corporeal World because the help which He was giving me was coming from the region which was beyond the sky. I only knew this much about Him before I began using the BK knowledge.

Since I have developed subtle abilities, I was able to see God in the subtle region, from the time I began hearing the Sakar Murli in the BK centers. One day, after I began making intense spiritual efforts based on the BK knowledge, I experienced God as being Mighty and Powerful. I was in His presence and I recognised that He was God. After the experience, I began to get worried about coming face to face with God because I felt that I have done so many wrong things and so:

1. I was wondering how an impure person like me can come before God.

2. I was worried that I will experience punishment for my sins.

The next morning, as I was listening to the Murli being read, after the early morning amrit vela meditation, I understood that we do not experience any punishment as our sins get burnt away during the Confluence Age. I also knew that God loves me just as He loves all His other children and that He is here to help us become pure again. God understands the situation which we are in, and He is trying to bring us out of this hell. I was very happy that I have found God and that I could now make spiritual efforts to *transform myself and my world* into the pure state.

During the Confluence Age, we know God in a practical way because we are in the subtle region with God. Many BKs might not be aware that they are in the presence of God since they do not have developed psychic abilities like me. However, the soul knows and so the BKs are influenced to think that they are with God. Their blissful experiences will also help them to know that they are with God.

Through my experiences, I know God in a practical way. During an experience, you (the soul) would also know when you are seeing God; you would recognise that it is God. After the experience, as the human being, you might not remember that you have been with the Father; however, as the soul, you will know that you have met God again and you (the deity soul) would be happy that you are now able to establish your perfect divine world again with God's assistance. To know God in a practical way, you have to keep creating elevated thoughts until your spiritual stage is high; so constantly keep creating elevated thoughts.

13   SHRIMAT (GODLY DICTATES)

Murli Extract (SM 24-12-2018):

"Consider yourself to be a soul and constantly remember Me alone. That's all! Simply follow the directions that I am giving you. You now have to renounce all the different dictates you have been following up to now. ...His second order is: While living at home with your family, remain as pure as a lotus. Only through the fire of yoga will your sins be burnt away."

Churning:

In the Murlis, you will find that God often tells you to do something and not to do something else; all these are shrimat (God's directions). The words 'directions' and 'order', in the above murli extract, are indications that these are God's shrimat.

Shrimat was given to help the BKs to become spiritual powerful. So, in the Brahma Kumaris, BKs follow shrimat. You should also follow them.

God gives directions based on who is sitting before Him when He is giving the Murli. His directions are also based on the requirements for that specific time. However, BKs attempt to follow all the directions that have been given by God because these will help to make us spiritually powerful.

The most important shrimat is to constantly see yourself as the soul while remembering only God/Baba. This is why, in His Murlis, God/Baba frequently gives directions to the effect "Consider yourself to be a soul" and "constantly remember Me alone". These most frequently repeated shrimat in the Murlis have to be obeyed so that you are able to establish a strong link to God. Thus, keep creating thoughts where you see yourself as the 'soul remembering God'.

So long as you are remembering the knowledge given by Baba, you are remembering Baba. For example, when you think about how the religion of the soul is peace, you are actually remembering that you are the soul and you are also remembering God since you are remembering the knowledge given by Him. Various kinds of thoughts, based on the BK knowledge, can be created during your attempts to remember Baba. These thoughts will automatically bring you into the soul conscious stage since they are thoughts based on the knowledge which is in the Murli.

Another important shrimat is to remain pure by living a pure lifestyle. This helps you to easily attain a high spiritual stage. Purity is the foundation of Brahmin life, and it is also the mother of peace and prosperity. While living a pure lifestyle, you have to keep making sure that your thoughts are pure elevated thoughts so that you remain linked to God. Through the exposure to God's powerful energies, your purity increases since:

1. your sins get burnt away, and

2. your impure energies transform into the pure state.

Baba gives shrimat so as to help you to transform into the pure divine state. When you follow Baba's shrimat, you easily stay linked to God and remain pure.

Murli Extract (SM 20-11-2018):

"You become pure by remembering the Father. The Father says: There is only one method for purification: forget all your bodily relations including your own body.

You know: I, the soul, have been given the order to have remembrance. By following this order, you will be called obedient. The more effort you make in this, the more obedient you become. If you have less remembrance, it means that you are less obedient. It is the obedient ones who claim a high status. The Father's first order is: Remember Me, your Father, and, secondly, imbibe this knowledge."

Churning:

Baba's first order/shrimat is to remember Him alone. One can only be purified through remembering Him. One does not become pure through remembering others or the body. When we obediently follow Baba's shrimat, we become spiritually powerful. As a result, we enjoy a higher status in the Golden Aged world.

Baba's second order/shrimat is to imbibe the knowledge given by Him in the Murlis. Through imbibing, we become soaked with the knowledge; hence, we become an embodiment of knowledge. This enables us to have a strong link to God. As a consequence, we receive more of God's powerful energies and there is greater purification. Whatever God tells us to do is for our own benefit. Therefore, keep a check on your thoughts to make sure that they are based on shrimat. This will help to you to imbibe the knowledge given by Baba.

14 BRAHMA, VISHNU, SHANKAR
AND THE LORD OF THE
THREE WORLDS

Murli Extract (SM 11-7-2018):

"You souls now know the Father. You children know
that Shiv Baba alone is the One who doesn't have a
subtle or a physical body. The subtle bodies of Brahma,
Vishnu and Shankar are shown. They are also given
names. You children understand that those subtle
bodies have a soul in them. At this time, you children
become lords of the three worlds. ...Brahma, Vishnu and
Shankar truly have subtle bodies. Shiva alone is
incorporeal. ...You children now know that you are
souls. The Supreme Father, the Supreme Soul, is
explaining to us children. He is giving us the knowledge
of the three worlds. At this time you are the lords of the
three worlds because you know them. Unless someone

knows the three worlds, how could he be a lord of them? ...Only Brahmins, the children of Brahma, are lords of the three worlds; they have knowledge of the three worlds. The Father is knowledge-full and blissful. That incorporeal Father is giving us knowledge. No corporeal human being can be called God. ...You now know the three worlds and this is why you are named trilokinath (lord of the three worlds). Only those who know about them could be their lords. You now have knowledge of the three worlds. Only you Brahmins know this."

Churning:

The three worlds that exist now are the Corporeal World, Angelic World and Soul World (Paramdham). The Angelic World, which is between the Corporeal World and the Soul World, only exists during the Confluence Age; it is only used by those who have accepted the BK knowledge for spiritual effort making purposes. The Angelic World consists of Brahmapuri, Vishnupuri and Shankarpuri.

Brahma, Vishnu and Shankar are subtle bodies which we use in the Angelic World. Since deity souls use these subtle bodies, there is a soul within those subtle bodies when we use them. Those subtle bodies only exist when we (the souls) use them. When we use those subtle bodies we are referred to by the names of Brahma,

Vishnu or Shankar, depending on which subtle body we use. We (the souls) will be in 2 worlds since we use the physical body in the Corporeal World and the subtle body of Brahma, Vishnu or Shankar in the Angelic World.

Create the thought that you are Shankar and you will be using the subtle body of Shankar. When you are Shankar you are in the very powerful stage of renunciation and tapasya (the surrendered, self-disciplined/austere, non-worldly, intense meditative state of Shankar). In this Shankar stage, you could also just experience yourself as the soul and might not be using a subtle body. You are in Shankarpuri when you are Skankar.

You are in Vishnupuri when you experience yourself as Vishnu, Laksmi or Narayan. Create the thought that you are Vishnu and you will be using the subtle body of Vishnu. You become what you think. So always have elevated thoughts about yourself; keep seeing yourself as Vishnu, Laksmi or Narayan.

When you contemplate on the BK knowledge, you will naturally be playing the role of Brahma in Brahmapuri and you will be using the subtle angelic body which God created for you (at the beginning of the Confluence Age) so that you can use it when you come into the Confluence Age. That angelic body only becomes the subtle body of Brahma when you begin to use it; so there will be a soul within the subtle body of Brahma.

We are involved with creating the new divine world through self-transformation, when we use this subtle body.

Normally, it is Brahma Baba who is referred to as Brahma. All the others, who use the BK knowledge, are referred to as Brahmins, the children of Brahma. All Confluence Aged souls are Brahmins because:

1. we are born via the knowledge that was given by God through the mouth of Brahma (Brahma Baba),

2. we are close to God (by virtue of our link to God), and

3. we help connect others to God.

When you accept the BK knowledge for spiritual effort making purposes, and use it, you are a Brahmin. Brahmins keep making spiritual efforts to remain in the Angelic World with God.

Since our physical bodies are used in the Corporeal World, human beings know a lot about this world. However, we do not really know everything about the Corporeal World, for example, we do not know how the state of the Corporeal World changes as time flows through each cycle. Further, non-BKs also do not know about the Angelic World and the Soul World. God has to give us the knowledge about all three worlds, through the Murlis, so that we can become trilokinath (lord of the three worlds). Since God has given us this knowledge, we know the three worlds.

Actually, it is the soul who becomes the lord of the three worlds. To become trilokinath you (the soul) have to accept the knowledge that is given by God about the three worlds, and you have to keep churning on them until you become an embodiment of knowledge. When you are an **embodiment of knowledge**, your mind, intellect and sanskaras are linked to God's Mind, Intellect and Sanskaras. Hence, you will know what God knows; you will know that the three worlds exist.

When you are saturated with the knowledge that is in the Murlis, you have experiences in respect of the three worlds; so you truly know about the three worlds. It is only through contemplating on the knowledge, which God has given in the Murlis, that you can have experiences of the three worlds and, thus, have knowledge of the three worlds in a practical way. During these experiences, you will know that the body is in the Corporeal World, that you (the soul) have been brought into the higher Angelic World and that the Soul World exists even higher up. To have these experiences, you will have to keep thinking about God and the knowledge which He has given until you are saturated with this knowledge.

You can have experiences even though you do not see visions. The visions are mainly for **guiding** you. You might **not** be in a spiritually powerful stage when you have a vision. You become spiritually powerful **when you have experiences** of the three worlds **while in the blissful stage**. When you are in this blissful stage, you are trilokinath because you will know that the three worlds (Corporeal World, Angelic World and Soul World) exist.

Actually, God is in the Angelic World during the Confluence Age; however, He still keeps a presence in the Soul World:

1. for the souls who have not come into the Corporeal World, and

2. so that we can have experiences of being in the Soul World.

When you are connected to God, you could have experiences of being in the Angelic World or Soul World since God resides in the Angelic World and Soul World. Through your **feelings**, you will know that you are in one of these worlds; you do **not** need a vision to become aware that you are in the Angelic World or Soul World.

We have truly understood the knowledge about the three worlds and are truly trilokinath:

1. when we have experiences of being in the Angelic World or/and Soul World.

2. if we experience ourselves as having a link to God who is in the Angelic World or/and Soul World.

3. when we get detached from the body and are able to see all three worlds, or know that all three worlds exist,

while we are in the blissful stage.

It is only through contemplating on the knowledge, which is given by God, that we can have such experiences. Thus, keep creating thoughts on the three worlds until you are saturated with these thoughts. This will help you to become an embodiment of knowledge and experience being trilokinath.

When contemplating on a murli point in respect of the three worlds, you can think about all that which has been said about the three worlds in the Murlis.

Murli extract (SM 5-12-2017):

"There are angels in the subtle region. That is the world of angels. Angels don't reside here. Deities are called deities. Those are angels whereas here, there are human beings. Everyone's section is separate. Deities rule in the golden age. That is the world of 'talkie'. The subtle region is the world of 'movie'. There are three worlds: the incorporeal world, the subtle region and the corporeal world. They speak of three worlds. You have this in your intellects in a practical way. ...You know all three worlds."

Churning:

The Golden Aged deities live in the Corporeal World just as we live in the Corporeal World. However, there are differences in the Golden Aged Corporeal World and the current Corporeal World.

The Angelic World is the Confluence Aged subtle region. We use our angelic bodies while we are in this subtle region. In this subtle region, no one talks like how we talk in the Corporeal World. We will be communicating subtly, in the subtle region, through the language of thoughts; everyone will know what the other is thinking.

When I am talking to someone (directly or over the phone), sometimes, when my spiritual stage is high, I see myself in the subtle region with that person and I will know what that person is thinking. If that person begins to talk through using the mouth, my consciousness immediately drops into the physical body/Corporeal World so that I can hear what the person is saying. Though we live in the Corporeal World, we can easily bring our consciousness into the subtle region through spiritual effort making. We can keep our consciousness in the subtle region even though we are using the body to see, hear, talk, carry out activities etc. Sometimes, we can completely bring our consciousness into the subtle region and not be aware of what is going on around the physical body. This happens during a split second experience; we do not completely remain in the subtle region for long. Thereafter, though we become aware of what is happening in the Corporeal World, our consciousness will remain in the subtle region if our spiritual stage is high. We are in the angelic stage during such times. We will have to keep making spiritual efforts to keep our consciousness in the subtle region even though we continue to use the physical body.

Constantly have the vision that you are residing in the Angelic World through persistently creating thoughts to this effect. You will be in the Angelic World when you have such elevated thoughts since they are based on the BK knowledge.

When you have experiences of being in the Angelic World or Soul World, impressions of these experiences are left in the energies of the soul. The intellect carries these impressions, and the knowledge about the three worlds, between the mind and memory bank when you keep remembering them; therefore, these will constantly be in your intellect. This keeps your intellect in an energised state. Ergo you can easily fly to the Angelic World to remain in God's Company. If you have not had any experiences as yet, begin to have them by intensely contemplating on the knowledge which is in the Murlis. Through intensely contemplating on any murli point, you can easily have experiences and you will know all three worlds in a practical way.

15   OM SHANTI

Murli Extract (SM 16-10-2018):

"Om shanti. The spiritual Father says to the spiritual
children: Children, om shanti. This is also called the
great mantra. The soul chants the mantra of his original
religion. The original religion of myself, the soul, is
peace. I don't need to go to the jungles etc. for peace. I,
the soul, am peaceful. ...There is a story about this: A
queen had her necklace around her neck, but she had
forgotten this and thought that her necklace was lost
and so she searched for it outside. Then someone told
her that her necklace was around her neck. This
example is given. ... However, the mind and intellect are
in the soul. When a soul receives these organs, he
comes into 'talkie'. The Father says: You souls should
remain stable in your original religion. Forget all the
religions of the body. ...Until the Father who can show

the path is found, no one is able to remain stable in the original religion."

Churning:

Om means "I, the soul". Om Shanti means "I, the soul, am an embodiment of peace". Peace is the original religion of the soul.

When you are in the soul conscious stage, you stabilise yourself in the original religion of the soul; so you experience peace, i.e. you are an embodiment of peace.

BKs say Om Shanti when they meet, or greet, each other and when they are about to leave each other's physical presence. The words 'Om Shanti' is a reminder to remain in the peaceful soul conscious stage; it is equivalent to creating the following thoughts:

1. I (the soul) am an embodiment of peace,

2. I (the soul) am the child of God (my Supreme Father who is an Ocean of Peace), and

3. I (the soul) am a resident of the Land of Peace (Soul World).

You (the soul) should keep remembering that you are the soul whose essence is peace. When you do this, it is as if you are chanting the mantra of the original religion of the soul. As a consequence, your thoughts resonate with the peaceful energies of the soul and Supreme Soul, and you become the embodiment of peace. You will be experiencing the peaceful vibrations of all the divine virtues and powers which you, the soul, are filled with. Peace is a virtue/power that includes all virtues and powers. Thus, being an embodiment of peace keeps you in a powerful state where you are filled with virtues and powers that are being empowered by God's Virtues and Powers.

You can also continuously keep creating the thought "Om Shanti" in your mind so that you become an embodiment of peace. When you fill your mind with this thought, you can become very powerful so long as it is reminding you that you are the peaceful soul who is linked to God. Through such a reminder, you (the soul) will become an embodiment of peace since you will be filled with God's powerful vibrations.

When you create the thought "Om Shanti" in your mind, you are actually contemplating on God's knowledge because these words were taught to us by God, through His Murlis. So you get the benefit of being exposed to God's Sounds of Silence which accompany these words. As a consequence, these words act like a mantra to empower you with peace; you get linked to God, become peaceful and enjoy peace. If the word 'Om' had meant something else, before you received the BK knowledge, you should reprogram yourself; keep remembering that 'Om' refers to you, the soul. The word 'Om' should only remind you that you are a soul.

It should also remind you of how God has given this knowledge to you. Then, the words 'Om' or 'Om Shanti' would act like a mantra that brings you into the soul conscious stage.

Whenever you say Om Shanti or hear this, you should remember that your original religion is peace and you should make sure that you are in the peaceful soul conscious stage. You need not be concerned about what is being taught in the various religions that exist in the world. You only have to make sure that you are stabilised in the religion of the soul: peace. When you are soul conscious, you remain stable in your original religion. So make spiritual efforts, through creating elevated thoughts, to enjoy the stage of being the embodiment of peace.

In the above Murli, the story about the necklace being around the queen's neck should remind you that you do not have to search everywhere for peace and happiness. Peace and happiness are there within you (the soul); just emerge them to enjoy them. When you create the thought that you are peaceful, you become peaceful. Similarly, when you create the thought that you are happy, you become happy because happiness is emerged into your mind based on your thought.

16   MIND, INTELLECT, SANSKARAS, CONTROLLING POWER, RULING POWER AND THE POWER OF COOLNESS

Murli Extract (AM 9-12-2018):

"According to the time and the situation, with your power of coolness, adjust the speed of your thoughts and words and make them cool and patient. If the speed of your thoughts is too fast, you waste a lot of time and cannot control them. Therefore, imbibe the power of coolness and save yourself from wastefulness and accidents. You will then be liberated from the fast speed of waste and of asking "Why? What? It should not be like this", etc. Sometimes, some children play big games. Waste thoughts come with so much force that they are unable to control themselves. Afterwards, they say "What can I do? It just happened!" They cannot stop themselves. They do whatever they want. However, you must gain power to control that waste. Just as you receive the fruit of multi-millions for one powerful thought, in the same way the fruit of one wasteful thought is sadness, disheartenment and the loss of your happiness. ...You need to have full rights over your subtle powers, your mind, your intellect and your sanskars. These powers are your special workers. These three special powers, your royal workers, are your main co-operative workers. When these three workers work on a signal that you, the soul, the king, the one with a right to the kingdom, give them, then your kingdom will constantly function correctly. A king doesn't do a task himself but gets it done by others. The one who does it is a servant of the king. If the king's servants do not serve him properly, then the kingdom starts to shake. You, the soul, gets things done; it is the special trimurti powers that do the work. First of all, you have to have ruling power over them. Your physical senses will then naturally move along accordingly on the right path. Just as it is said of the golden-aged kingdom that there is one kingdom and one religion, in the same way, in your own kingdom, there now has to be one king. That is, let everything function according to your directions. Your mind should not function according to its own directions; your intellect's power of discernment should not fluctuate; your sanskars should not make you, the soul, dance. It can then be said that you have one religion, one kingdom. Imbibe such controlling power.

In order to pass with honours and claim all rights to the kingdom, you need to have total control over the subtle power of your mind. Your mind must do everything according to your orders. Whatever you think should be on your orders. If you say, "Stop!" it should stop. If you say, "Think about service!" it should become engaged in service. If you say, "Think about Paramdham!", you should reach Paramdham. Now, increase such controlling power. Do not waste time battling over trivial matters."

Churning:

Your mind, intellect and sanskaras (memory bank) consist of the energies of the soul. They are you (the soul); hence, when something is done with the assistance of the mind, intellect and sanskaras, you can have the experience that you are doing it. This is also why you feel that you are creating your thoughts. Actually, **you are** creating your thoughts; however, you are using your mind to create those thoughts. It can also be said that your mind creates those thoughts for you since it is the thinking faculty of the soul. All thoughts are created within the mind and your mind serves you by creating these thoughts for you. Your mind, intellect and sanskaras are your workers, ministers or subtle powers.

Before you received this knowledge, your mind might

have been creating negative or waste thoughts on its own even though you (the soul) were not taking the initiative to create those thoughts. You probably would have had the habit of creating numerous negative/waste thoughts too. Through using the knowledge in the Murlis, you would be changing this habit so that you keep creating elevated thoughts out of habit. You change the bad habit of creating negative/waste thoughts by changing the way you think. Your new thinking process should only consist of having elevated thoughts in your mind. You have to take control over the kind of thoughts that get created in your mind so as to become spiritually powerful. Your mind should no longer create thoughts on its own:

1. based on the old habits of creating negative/waste thoughts,

2. due to a weak state, or

3. due to influences from the vices.

The vices are taking control and, for this reason, negative/waste thoughts are getting created in your mind. These impure energies have to be transformed back into the pure energies through being exposed to God's energies, and you will also have to make sure that waste/negative thoughts are not created within your mind.

When you establish the habit of creating thoughts based on the knowledge in the Murlis, you will keep creating such elevated thoughts out of habit. They get created because you want to habitually think in this way. This new habit will help to keep you in a spiritually high stage. It involves sanskar transformation, i.e. changing the old bad devilish sanskars into new divine sanskaras or habits.

When your mind, intellect and sanskaras are under your control, only elevated thoughts will get created in your mind. However, since you have not become spiritually powerful, by virtue of making spiritual efforts over a long period of time, the vices and old habits can influence you. So you should make sure that the 'old habits of creating negative/waste thoughts' do not create waste/negative thoughts in your mind. When you have control over the thoughts which get created in your mind, you have *controlling power* and *ruling power* over your mind.

Your intellect should also not bring information/memories into your mind, from the memory bank (sanskaras), if you did not have the intent to consider those information/memories. When the intellect is in a weak state, it will bring all sorts of information from the memory bank, even though you did not have the intention to consider them. In addition, when your intellect is weak, your intellect's power of discernment is weak; ergo, you will not be able to use it properly for making decisions. When your intellect's power of discernment is weak, you will find yourself in a confused state since you will find it difficult to make good and appropriate decisions. When you are a Confluence Aged spiritual effort maker and are in a high spiritual stage, you will be using your divine intellect since your intellect transforms from the weak ordinary state to the powerful divine state through being empowered by God's energies. As a consequence, your intellect's power of discernment can be accurately used for making very good decisions. You will have to make sure that your intellect's power of discernment does not fluctuate by keeping a check on your thoughts. You have to ensure that there are no negative/waste thoughts in your mind and that your thoughts are only elevated thoughts. When your thoughts are elevated, you will be in a high stage and, similarly, your intellect will be in a powerful state. If there are negative/waste thoughts in your mind, your intellect will be in a weak state.

Your memories/information should also not be emerging as they like, from the memory bank, due to a weak state. If you do not have controlling power, your sanskaras/memories would be emerging uncontrollably from the memory bank and this would be influencing the way you think and act; you will lose control over the activities you do and the way you think. When you only have elevated thoughts in your mind, you will have a high spiritual stage. For this reason, your sanskaras will be under your control; only information which you want, or need, will be emerged by the intellect.

When your spiritual stage is very high, you can easily

stop negative/waste thoughts with just an order, through your thought, that you should stop thinking these negative/waste thoughts. When you have the thought that you should stop thinking these negative/waste thought, you will definitely stop doing it if:

1. you have become spiritually powerful by making spiritual efforts over a long period of time.

2. you have changed the way you think.

3. you have been constantly making intense spiritual efforts during that day and during the few days before that.

When you are able to stop thinking negatively with just a thought that you should stop it, your mind, intellect and sanskaras are under your control; so your mind stops creating negative thoughts, your intellect does not bring negativity/waste into the mind, and your impure memories would not be emerging into your mind on their own. If you had the thought to only think about service, you would only think about service. If you had the thought to only think about God residing in Paramdham (Soul World), you will only be thinking about that; so you will have an experience of being in Paramdham with God.

When you have controlling power over your mind, intellect and sanskaras, you have ruling power over them. To have controlling power, you have to keep making spiritual efforts, over a long duration of time, to become spiritually powerful. The more powerful you (the soul) become, the greater your controlling power. You will be imbibing controlling power through spiritual effort making; therefore you accumulate controlling power as you keep making spiritual efforts. The greater your controlling power, the greater your ruling power.

You will also have controlling power and ruling power when you are in a high spiritual stage. When you are in a spiritually high stage, you will have ruling power because you will be seated on your seat/throne in the center of the forehead. Your mind, intellect and sanskaras will function well since they are in the pure divine state. When you have controlling power and ruling power, you are a self-sovereign, a Raja Yogi who is in yoga with God. You, the soul, will be a ruler over yourself. Since the mind, intellect and sanskaras carry out your orders, you will be a king in this kingdom that is within you (the soul). You will be stabilised in the religion of the soul too.

Always have the thought that you have controlling power and ruling power over your mind, intellect and sanskaras. When you have this thought, they will be under your control. You will have to keep them under your control so as to become spiritually powerfully. Then, you will be able to claim all rights to rule in the Golden Aged kingdom and you will be a self-sovereign now. When you have control over your mind, intellect and sanskaras, you will also have control over the 5 senses (taste, sight, touch, sound and smell). So keep a check on your thoughts at every moment in time.

Negative/waste thoughts are normally uncontrollable thoughts. When there is just one negative/waste thought in your mind, the waste will multiply intensively; so there will be numerous negative/waste thoughts in your mind. The speed of creation of these thoughts is fast and it can be very difficult to stop such thoughts when one is in a weak state. Trying to stop such thoughts, while in a weak state, might only amplify them and make it worse. To stop them, you will have to keep your mind preoccupied with thoughts on the knowledge given by Baba/God.

Through intensely contemplating on the BK knowledge, you imbibe the power of coolness. The negative/waste thoughts can be overcome via this power of coolness. You imbibe the power of coolness when:

1. your spiritual stage is high, and

2. you are not burning due to being overcome by the vices.

With the power of coolness, you can make others cool as well if they are burning due to being overwhelmed by the vices. One is filled with divine love when one has the power of coolness. Hence, one can easily keep oneself cool and influence others to become cool.

You should make yourself spiritually powerful so that

waste thoughts do not exist in your mind and you do not get hurt in anyway due to indulging in wasteful thoughts. When you make spiritual efforts, the speed of your thoughts will slow down because elevated thoughts, based on God's knowledge, will slow down the speed of your thoughts. You will no longer be indulging in negative/waste thoughts because they cannot exist in your mind when your spiritual stage is high. Then, you will only be capable of thinking elevated thoughts. Each elevated thought is very powerful; the fruit you enjoy (through the Law of Karma), for each elevated thought, is a multi-million fold. By only entertaining elevated thoughts, you enjoy bliss now and you will enjoy living a heavenly life in the Golden Aged world. In contrast, if you had negative/waste thoughts in your mind, you can experience uncontrollable sadness and it can seem like you are living in hell because these negative/waste thoughts will automatically influence you to indulge in the vices.

You must attempt to only have a few thoughts which are based on the BK knowledge. You will have fewer thoughts when your spiritual stage is high. The fewer the thoughts you have, the more powerful your spiritual stage.

Hold an elevated thought in your mind for as long as you can. This will increase your power of concentration. This thought can be a murli point or any thought that is based on the BK knowledge. If you are churning on a murli point, you can think about all aspects of that murli point. However, try to make sure that your thoughts are only about that murli point so that you only entertain a few powerful thoughts based on a murli point. This helps to improve your power of concentration. You can easily go into a high spiritual stage if you have a developed power of concentration. If you feel restricted, while limiting your thoughts to one or a few, then allow yourself to just think anything so long as it is only about the knowledge given by God or about God's service. Your power of concentration can be developed over time as you keep improving the way you think.

Murli Extract (AM 17-1-2016):

"Maya cannot come to those who have ruling power. When Maya sees that all of your workers are very wise and are all paying full attention, she doesn't have the courage to go near them."

Churning:

When you are in a high spiritual stage, Maya (negative/waste thoughts) would not dare emerge to influence you because, if they emerge, they will get burnt away by God's energies which are within you (the soul). Maya also cannot emerge when your stage is high because you can only be in a pure state when your spiritual stage is high. Maya can only emerge when you are losing your high stage, or just before you attain your stage, so as to try to keep you under the influence and control of the vices. For this reason, when you are making spiritual efforts to attain a high spiritual stage, you have to keep a close watch on what kind of thoughts exists in your mind.

17 DETACHED OBSERVER AND TIME TO RETURN HOME

Murli Extract (SM 19-10-18):

"The Father says: You may live at home, but it should remain in your intellects that you have to return home. When a play is about to end, the actors become detached from the play. While playing their parts, their intellects are aware that a short time remains and that, after playing their parts, they will return home. You too have to keep it in your intellects that it is now the end. We are now going into divine relationships. While living in this old world, it should remain in your intellects that you are going to the Father... Baba repeatedly tells you: Consider yourselves to be souls. We now have to return home. All the actors are playing their own parts; they will shed their bodies and return home. You just have to observe as detached observers."

Churning:

When you see yourself as the soul ready to return Home (to the Soul World) with Baba/God, you become soul conscious. While in the soul conscious stage, you are detached from your body and you observe everything as a detached observer, i.e. you (the soul) will watch everything as if you are watching a drama or movie. When you observe something as a detached observer, you are not influenced by what you see, hear, smell, touch, etc. You will watch everything as an actor who is aware that it is now time to return Home; you will not have any attachment to anyone nor be affected by the impurity that surrounds you. Since your spiritual stage is high, you will not react to what you see, hear, etc. You will remain in a happy, peaceful, virtuous state no matter what happens around you.

Further, what you are watching will not create impure memories/impressions within the soul, when your spiritual stage is high, since the impressions will be left on pure powerful energies. It will not be a karm bandhan (bondage of karma), it will be a karm yoga (remembrance of God whilst doing karma); so a different kind of impression is left within the soul and there will be an accumulation of powerful energies within the memory bank of the soul. If you do not watch everything as a detached observer, impressions will be left on the weak ordinary energies of the soul and these weak energies will become impure energies since impurities are left as impressions on these energies of the soul. This, in turn, will increase the impurities within the soul.

When you recollect these memories, another thought/impression is created based on what is being remembered and this thought/impression would be left on the weak energies of the soul **if your spiritual stage is not high**; these weak energies of the soul will become impure energies due to being exposed to impurities. As a consequence, impure energies will accumulate within the memory bank of the soul. These impure memories will also influence you in a negative way, bringing you into a unhappy state. So be very careful when you have to recollect something; make sure that you are in a powerful spiritual stage so that further impressions of the memories are not left on the weak energies of the soul.

Through constantly remembering that it is now time to return Home:

1. you will understand (by way of experiences) the importance of remembering Baba and the knowledge which He has given.

2. you will easily go into the soul conscious stage.

3. you will find it easy to remain in the detached observer stage, and will only have a close relationship

with God, because you know that you are only playing a role, as per the world drama. You will play your role well, in the lokik family, through making every lokik family member happy and contended, by absorbing and sending God's vibrations to them. There would not be any bondage but only a duty to keep them in the pure state through absorbing and sending them God's vibrations.

For your own benefit and for the benefit of everyone else, constantly keep remembering that it is time to return home and see yourself as an actor who is ready to go back Home with God. All the thoughts which you create should be those of one who is a detached observer so that you become spiritually powerful. When we become spiritually powerful, we are close to God when we return Home. So constantly have the aim to become spiritually powerful through creating elevated thoughts.

18   CYCLE OF TIME AND MASTER ALMIGHTY AUTHORITY

Murli Extract (SM 19-11-2018):

"This eternal world drama continues to rotate. You children know this."

Churning:

When thinking about a murli point on the cycle, you can think about all that which God has said in respect of what happens during each cycle, including on how the Golden Age, Silver Age, Copper Age, Iron Age (Kaliyug) and Confluence Age (Sangamyug) keep repeating exactly during every cycle. You can think about how what you are doing now is what happens at the end of each cycle and how you have to make intense spiritual efforts because it is time for all souls to return Home with God.

When you keep churning on the knowledge that God gives, whether it is on the cycle or on some other murli point, God will give you various experiences, including on the cycle, so as to help you to have a better understanding on the knowledge. However, it will be easier to have an experience on the cycle, if you kept contemplating on it.

Sometime around 1998, when I was intensely making spiritual efforts and churning on my part in the cycle, I had an experience on how the eternal world drama keeps repeating as the cycle continues to rotate. My subtle form was brought into the higher subtle region and I could see the BK Cycle of Time (spinning in a cyclic manner) before me. I could see time flowing in a cyclic manner. I knew that this cycle was rotating eternally and I knew that the world drama that was taking place in the cycle also repeated eternally. This helped me to have faith that the world drama does keep repeating in a cyclic manner.

I had this experience when I was making intense spiritual efforts, during my lunch hour, in a legal firm which I was working in. From that morning until the lunch break, I had frequently taken a few seconds off, once in a while, to think about how it is now the end of the cycle and I had to earn money to go and meet Baba in Madhuban. I had thought about the cycle, from the view that I was now at the end of the cycle when Baba has come to create the new divine world for us. I wanted to take my next birth at the beginning of the Golden Age and I wanted to be a world emperor in that birth; I was keeping this aim in my mind while making intense efforts and remembering God. Thinking intensely, about the cycle and God, gave me this wonderful experience where I knew that the world drama does continue to rotate eternally. The fact that I had this experience while I was at my **work place** shows that we can have good experiences anywhere so long as our thoughts are accurate. We just have to do our job with the proper mind-set. Accurate thoughts, etc. are needed to have a proper mind-set.

Murli Extract (SM 20-11-2018):

"The past, present and future are called the beginning, the middle and the end of the world. I know the repetition of this cycle, how it repeats. I come to teach you children this knowledge. ...Now the Father says: By knowing Me, you will come to know everything. Only I explain the knowledge of the beginning, the middle and the end of the world."

Churning:

In my abovementioned experience on how the cycle keeps spinning, I knew what the beginning, middle and the end of the cycle were like. Actually, I knew what happens throughout the cycle. However, the most significant times are during the beginning, middle and end of the cycle because these are the times when the world transforms from one state to another.

During my abovementioned experience, I was in a very high spiritual stage because I was making intense spiritual effort to attain a high stage that whole day from the time of amrit vela (early morning hours). In fact, I was making intense spiritual efforts from 1996. During the experience, I was in a high blissful stage and I was observing the spinning cycle as a detached observer. God was teaching me through this experience. This is the benefit of having God as our Teacher. When I came back into my body, I knew that whatever God has explained about the cycle, in the Murlis, was the truth. Many souls have experiences but after the experience, when they come back into the body, they might not remember what they saw as the soul. The soul would know but as the person they do not remember what they had experienced because they do not have the psychic ability to remember when they come back into the body. However, since the soul had the experience, the person would find it easy to accept the knowledge which God has given about the cycle.

As you churn on the knowledge, which are in the Murlis, you have to absorb the knowledge so as to experience being an embodiment of knowledge. This was how I had that experienced. At the point when I was an embodiment of knowledge, I knew that what God has said is true.

If you have not had any experiences on the cycle, you might find it difficult to accept the 5000 year cycle because you have not spiritually understood that this is true. Therefore, you have to keep churning the knowledge so that you have knowledge of the cycle in a practical way.

Murli Extract (AM 29/05/16):

"BapDada gives each of you children the experience of your final stage, that is, the complete and perfect stage, the powerful stage. In this stage, you constantly experience: being a master almighty authority, a master sun of knowledge and complete with all virtues, being a detached observer in every thought, every breath and at every second, being a constant companion of the Father, and receiving the companionship of the love and co-operation of all the elevated souls of the Brahmin family."

Churning:

A master almighty authority is one who is experiencing a high **powerful stage** where one knows that the knowledge that has been given by God is the truth. During that experience:

1. one has all powers, and

2. one is an authority on the knowledge that is given by God.

God knows that the knowledge, which He has given us, is the truth and He is 'One with all Powers'; hence, He is the Almighty Authority. When we know that it is the truth while we are in a powerful state, we are the master almighty authority because we are the children of God. God gives us the experience and we become a master almighty authority.

During my abovementioned experience on the cycle spinning eternally, I was in the stage of being a master almighty authority. This has influenced me, thereafter, to accept the knowledge on the cycle as the truth. In fact, it has made me accept everything, which Baba has said, as the truth. Just thinking about this experience helps me to go into a high spiritual stage since the impressions of the experience are left on powerful divine energies. It is a treasure within me that keeps influencing me until now. One is in the high soul conscious stage when one has such experiences.

While we are in a high stage:

1. all souls, including the BKs, will be co-operative,

2. we would be co-operating with other BKs to maintain a powerful gathering, and

3. we would be able to experience being in the subtle company of BKs who are in the powerful stage (though we do not see subtle beings through visions). We would have the experience that we are in a powerful gathering; this gathering was established by virtue of the love and co-operation of all the elevated souls of the Brahmin family. You would feel that you belong this spiritual family.

If you make intense spiritual efforts over a long duration of time, God/Baba will give you an experience too because you are also His child. All you need to do is to keep a check on your thoughts and make sure that they are based on the BK knowledge.

19   MAYA RAVAN

Murli Extract (SM 10-10-2018):

"There are five vices in the female and five vices in the male. That is the Ravan community. ...Ravan is the vices."

Churning:

Ravan/Ravana (the demon king) represents the five vices: anger, lust, greed, attachment and ego. These five vices influence us to indulge in the vices and negative/waste thinking.

In the Hindu myths, Ravan has been portrayed as having 10 heads: five of these heads represent the 5 vices in women and the other 5 heads represent the 5 vices in men. Ravan with the 10 heads represents how the vices, in men and women, rule the world in the second half cycle.

The vices of all human beings (collectively) form a collective consciousness which is the Devil/Ravana. This evil collective consciousness acts as one (Ravana) so that the vices can remain in control. Hence, if you try to remain pure, others, who are consumed by the vices, will try to bring you out of this pure path so that you will start yielding to the vices again.

Keep creating pure elevated thoughts based on the knowledge in the Murlis and keep sending God's energies into the world so that Maya-Ravan can be completely removed from the face of the earth.

Murli Extract (SM 13-2-2018):

"The kingdom of Ravan begins with the copper age."

Churning:

At the end of the Silver Age, the energies of the soul transformed into the weak ordinary state and these ordinary energies could transform into the vices. Thus, the kingdom of Ravana began from the beginning of the Copper Age.

From the time of the Copper Age, the rule of Ravana became increasingly stronger because we were indulging in the vices. When the vices are given free rein to, more of your energies transform into the vices. Therefore, you give Ravana greater control in the world.

Baba has now come to recreate the Golden Aged kingdom and to bring an end to the kingdom of Ravana. So we should be assisting God through only creating elevated thoughts. We have to keep a check on our thoughts to make sure that we are not yielding to the vices.

Murli Extract (SM 23-7-2018):

"Their war is one of violence whereas your war is with Ravan in the form of the five vices. You know that you have been following shrimat every cycle. At this time the whole world is following the dictates of Ravan. By following shrimat you become deities, those with divine directions. You now belong to the Brahmin clan. You make the whole world pure from impure. ...You know that the Father is now liberating you from Maya, Ravan. ...The battle of you children is with Maya, Ravan."

Churning:

The word 'Maya' (the female demon) is used to represent the vices at the thought level, i.e. when no action is taken, based on the thoughts, through using the physical body. Maya includes all waste thoughts, memories of sinful actions that disturb you, negative thoughts and all other impure thoughts which are created based on the influence of the vices. These weaken you and bring you under the control of vices. When one takes an action or actions, due to the influence of the impure thoughts, then the vices are referred to as Ravana or Ravan. The fact that you have been influenced to take actions is an indication that the vices, which influenced you, are stronger. The vices in the stronger form are referred to as Ravana and the vices in the milder or subtler form (which are only at thought level) are referred to as Maya.

In the Murlis, the vices are generally referred to as Ravana/Ravan. The word 'Maya Ravan' is used to refer to both: the vices and the negative/waste thoughts that get created based on the influence of the vices.

The vices, and thoughts that are created based on the vices, are impure and unrighteous. Hence, Maya Ravan has to be removed from the face of the earth. The vices, and the thoughts which are created through the influence of the vices, are unrighteous because:

1. the vices are energies that are not in the original pure state.

2. you are harming yourself (soul and body) when you are overwhelmed by the vices. The vices and negative thoughts are generally destructive in nature; for this reason, they affect the soul and body in a detrimental manner.

The presence of Maya Ravan in your mind is also inauspicious since it is an indication that you are not having a strong link to God. Since they will prevent you from having a strong link to God, make sure that there are no negative/waste thoughts in your mind and also keep a check on how you feel.

We should no longer follow the dictates of Ravan because we are Brahmins acting as instruments of God for the transformation of the impure world into the pure world. After this, all deity souls take births in the first half cycle and they follow the divine directions of the world rulers because Ravana no longer exists. However, now, we have to follow shrimat so as to become victorious over the vices.

Since Confluence Aged souls are transforming themselves back into the pure righteous state, they have to battle with Maya Ravan so as to remain in control. We make sure that impure thoughts are destroyed at the level of thoughts and no actions are taken due to their influence. We try to remain in a high stage so that the vices dare not come near. If the vices come into our minds when our spiritual stage is high, they will get burnt away by means of the fire of yoga with God. However, when you are beginning your spiritual efforts, and you have not attained a high stage as yet, Maya Ravan will try its best to keep you in the impure state by trying to influence you in whatever way it can. Thus, when you are trapped in negative thinking, and you are trying to push away the negative thoughts, the negative thoughts can get amplified. This happens because the vices will be struggling harder to overpower you. It can seem like a battle is taking place between the virtuous you and the devil (the vices). You will have to fight a very fierce battle to keep your mind in a pure state so that you can attain a high spiritual stage. However, just think of Baba and absorb His vibrations, and you will win the battle against Maya Ravan with ease.

When you are first introduced to the BK knowledge and you start making spiritual efforts, you will easily attain a pure spiritual stage. However, with time, the vices will become aware of what is happening and they will try harder to remain in control. You will have to become an intense effort maker, to make sure that you are not defeated by Maya. You can overcome all the challenges of Maya, which you face, through just contemplating on the knowledge which God has given. You will surely become victorious because God is with you during that churning process.

You will find it difficult to link yourself to God if you are indulging in the vices. Thus, make sure that there are no vices or impure thoughts in your mind, when you meditate. You should only be having thoughts on the BK knowledge in your mind.

If you keep a proper check over what kind of thoughts exists in your mind, you would be unassailed by waste/negative thoughts which Maya Ravan throw at you. You have to make sure that you are not influenced by impure thoughts and do not take any actions based on the influence of the vices.

While the wars of other people involve violence, our war is only against Maya Ravan. This means that, through spiritual effort making, we are making ourselves pure and, as a consequence, we are also creating a pure world where the vices do not exist. We are able to do this because God/Baba has come to liberate us from Maya Ravan. By absorbing God's energies into us, we can transform the energies of the vices back into the pure divine state; the world transforms as we transform and, through this, Maya Ravan is defeated.

Keep creating thoughts to the effect that you are a powerful soul who is constantly victorious over the vices because this will bring you into a pure powerful stage; it will help you to gain victory over Maya Ravan. Keep remembering that we defeated Maya Ravan at the end of every previous cycle, so there will undoubtedly be a triumphant victory even now. We are the incognito warriors of God, so we will definitely be victorious in the subtle war against Maya Ravan.

Murli Extract (AM 29-4-18):

"Constantly keep yourself under the canopy of the Father's protection. Those who stay under the canopy of protection become constant conquerors of Maya. If you don't stay under the canopy of protection, if you are sometimes under it and sometimes away from it, you are defeated. Those who stay under the canopy of protection don't have to make effort. The rays of all powers automatically make you conquerors of Maya. The awareness of, 'The one Father belongs to me in all relationships,' makes you a powerful soul."

Churning:

When you absorb God's energies into you, via your link to God, you are under God's canopy of protection. The vices, including negative/waste thoughts, would not dare emerge into the mind because they will get burnt away by God's energies which are protecting you while purifying you. You should only have a close relationship with Baba because this will make it very easy for you to stay under God's canopy of protection. When you keep creating thoughts about the knowledge given by Baba and keep remembering Him, you will have God's canopy of protection and your relationship with God strengthens with time.

20   SPIRITUAL INCOME

Murli Extract (AM 19-8-2018):

"Just have one powerful thought or perform one powerful deed and through that one seed, you attain multimillion-fold fruit."

Churning:

Through just one powerful thought or deed (done for this Confluence Aged Godly service) you will be able to earn a huge spiritual income that can be enjoyed:

1. now (through stability, happiness, peace, purity, etc.)

2. in the first half cycle (through wealth, status, purity, peace, happiness, etc). We claim this inheritance now,

during the Confluence Age, by transforming ourselves into the divine state. Thus, we can take births in the first half cycle to enjoy wealth, status, happiness, etc.

Through a powerful thought, we attain a high spiritual stage due to establishing a powerful link to God. As a consequence, we absorb God's energies to transform ourselves into the divine state. Since this transformation process helps to transform the whole world, we earn a huge spiritual income, via the Law of Karma, for this. Since a multimillion-fold benefit is given to the whole world, through our spiritual effort making, the spiritual income which we earn is a multimillion-fold. This is the fruit of our spiritual effort making during the Confluence Age.

Every act which we do as service for establishing the Golden Aged world, will also help us to earn a huge spiritual income. Therefore, we should constantly think about how we can do service that will help to establish the Golden Aged world.

The Confluence Age is the season when we can easily earn a huge spiritual income by means of remembering *God/Baba and the knowledge which He has given* and through doing service. You can only earn such a huge income during the Confluence Age, so don't miss this opportunity. Make sure that you do not doubt the knowledge because this weakens your thoughts. Have faith that God is teaching you because this will help you to create powerful thoughts.

Murli Extract (SM 13-10-2018):

"Look at the income on the path of devotion and the income on the path of knowledge! Baba fills your treasure-store completely. It takes effort. You definitely have to remain pure."

Churning:

The charity that is done by non-BKs do not earn as much, through the Law of Karma, as the spiritual effort-making and service done by BKs because we are involved with world transformation. Further, we are concerned about earning a spiritual income whereas non-BKs are mainly concerned about earning a monetary income that is perishable and can only be enjoyed in their present birth. Our spiritual income fills our treasure store within the soul and we can enjoy the fruits of the accumulated spiritual income during all our births in the heavenly world of the first half cycle.

Through contemplating on the knowledge given by Baba/God and remembering Baba, your treasure-store (within the soul) gets filled with:

1. divine virtues and powers,

2. knowledge, and

3. spiritual income.

The more you remember the knowledge and God, the more your treasure-store gets filled with all the abovementioned spiritual treasures. To get your treasure-store filled, you have to make sure that you are not indulging in impurities, for example, make sure that your thoughts are elevated thoughts that are based on the knowledge in the Murlis.

Do not indulge in the vices and negative thinking. Keep thinking about how lucky you are to be given this opportunity to accumulate such spiritual treasures. Have the aim to accumulate as much spiritual treasures as possible. When you have this aim, your thinking process will change to accommodate this aim.

21 CLAIMING YOUR INHERITANCE

Murli Extract (SM 18-10-18):

"You are claiming your inheritance from Shiv Baba. So
you have to remember Him alone. It is by having
remembrance that your burden of sins will be removed.
You know that this is the vicious impure world. The
golden age is the viceless world. There is no poison
(vice) there. According to the system, everyone only has
one son. There is never untimely death there; it is the
land of happiness. Here, there is so much sorrow. ...I
have come to take everyone back home. I am teaching
you so that you become the masters of heaven. You
know that, at this time, all human beings are constantly
unfortunate. In the golden age, you were constantly
fortunate. ...The Father now explains to you: I am
making you children become like Lakshmi and Narayan.
Have the faith that you are claiming your inheritance

from Baba and then, in the future, you will become princes and princesses. ...The Father says: Remember Me and your sins will be absolved and you will receive wings with which to fly. You are now changing from those with stone intellects into those with divine intellects. The Creator, the Father of all, is only One. ...The Father is the Liberator, the Remover of Sorrow and the Bestower of Happiness. ...You claim the kingdom every cycle and then lose it. ...Sorrow begins in the copper age. The Father says: I come and change the residents of hell into residents of heaven. ...You are being made into the masters of heaven by the unlimited Father and so your mercury of this happiness should rise."

Churning:

When we remember Baba, our sins are burnt away and we become pure. Through this remembrance, we also claim our inheritance.

In the present Confluence Aged spiritual birth, the inheritance which we enjoy is: all the virtues and powers, spiritual income (which increases our spiritual strength), purity, etc. As the virtues, powers, etc. increase within us, we experience greater bliss, stability, etc.

One earns a huge spiritual income through making

spiritual efforts because the world transforms into the divine state as we transform. The spiritual income which gets accumulated, within the soul, determines what we enjoy in the first half cycle. The greater the spiritual income and spiritual strength of the soul, the greater the status, wealth, happiness, etc. which we enjoy in our births taken during the first half cycle. We claim our inheritance from God/Baba now to enjoy wealth, status, happiness, the divine state etc. in the future births which we take in the Golden and Silver Ages; we would be able to live in a viceless world where:

1. there is no untimely death.

2. everyone only experiences happiness.

3. we are constantly fortunate.

4. we are the masters of heaven.

5. we are Lakshmi (the Golden Aged world empress) or Narayan (the Golden Aged world emperor).

Through remembering Baba we become light and our intellect can easily fly to the Angelic World. Through this we transform into the divine state and claim our inheritance.

Baba "is the Liberator, the Remover of Sorrow and the Bestower of Happiness" since He transforms the old world into the **new divine world** and takes all souls back

Home to the Soul World. However, the world can only get transformed into the divine world if we claim our inheritance now. We have to transform so that the world transforms. As we transform, we claim our inheritance from God.

To make sure that you receive a huge inheritance which can be enjoyed, from the beginning of the Golden Age, as princes and princesses:

1. keep thinking about how fortunate you are to be able to claim your inheritance now.

2. constantly keep remembering your aim which is to claim your inheritance now.

3. have faith that you are claiming an unlimited inheritance from Baba now.

The inheritance which you receive from your worldly/lokik father is limited and perishable. It can only be enjoyed in this birth. The inheritance which you claim from your parlokik Father is unlimited and it can be enjoy during so many births from the Golden Age onwards. To claim your inheritance now from the Supreme Father, change the way you think.

22   REMEMBERING GOD AND THE CYCLE TO BECOME WORLD RULERS

Murli Extract (SM 17-9-2018):

"By you remembering the Father, the whole cycle enters your intellect. By turning the cycle around in your intellect you will become rulers of the globe."

Churning:

You know that God has come and given the BK knowledge because it is the end of the cycle. Hence, even though you are not actually contemplating on the cycle and are only remembering God, your intellect will be having all the knowledge/memories, of how and why God came, within it. This is because the intellect collects all relevant memories, when you think of something, so as to bring them into your mind. The cycle is also a relevant memory when you remember God because God comes, at the end of each cycle, **to bring in the new cycle**, as a consequence of which you are able to claim your inheritance. Therefore, the whole cycle is in your intellect when you remember Baba.

When you churn on the cycle, you are a spinner of the discus of self-realisation (Swadarshanchakradhari). In my abovementioned experience where I saw the cycle spinning eternally, while I was churning on my role in the cycle, I was a Swadarshanchakradhari. I knew that I was the soul who eternally participates in that world drama cycle, just as everyone else does.

The process of churning on the cycle represents the spinning swadarshan chakra that cuts the throat of Maya Ravan; as a consequence of which you will be able to take your next birth in the Golden Age. For your own benefit, you should keep churning on the cycle so as to bring about the demise of Maya Ravan. You just have to keep contemplating on how you have taken so many births during the different Ages of the cycle, and have finally come into the Confluence Age. You think about how you (the soul) were slowly losing your spiritual strength during every birth in the cycle until the Confluence Age when you take a high jump to become spiritually powerful. You think about how the state of the soul and person changes throughout the cycle. This churning will help you to have relevant experiences. You (the person) might not remember what you had seen as the soul, during the experience, but you will be able to accept the knowledge on the cycle and this will help you to become spiritually powerful. As a result, you become ready for world transformation and so Maya Ravan will be completely exterminated from the face of the earth. Then, you will take births in the Golden Age where the rulers are world rulers.

You have to make a lot of spiritual efforts to become a ruler of the globe, in the Golden Age. So keep remembering Baba and the cycle.

23 KNOWLEDGE-FULL SEED OF THE HUMAN WORLD TREE

Murli Extract (SM 20-11-2018):

"He is the knowledge-full Seed of the human world tree."

Churning:

God is the knowledge-full Seed of the human world tree because:

1. He has the complete knowledge of the human world tree, i.e. He is filled with the full knowledge of what happens in the human world tree, and His never forgets this knowledge like how we forget it. He comes, at the

end of the cycle, and makes us aware of the knowledge which we have forgotten.

2. He has knowledge of the past, present and future, which happens in the world tree, to a **greater extent** than we. Through linking ourselves to Him, we will be able to have a better understanding of the human world tree since our mind, intellect and sanskaras connect to His Mind, Intellect and Sanskaras.

3. He has the whole treasure of knowledge within Him; this is given to us so as to bring in the new human world tree.

4. the **new human world tree grows** through our remembrance of the Seed (God) and the knowledge given by Him. The human world tree, which human beings play their part in, is an expansion of the knowledge that is within the Seed (God) since it grows based on our churning this knowledge.

Each murli point, which the knowledge-full Seed (God) has given, helps to bring in the new world tree when we churn on it. When you have just a murli point in your mind, you are linked to God's entire treasure and you will be able to understand the knowledge given by God, including the knowledge on the world tree. That murli point (or thought on the murli point) is like the seed that links you to the knowledge-full Seed (God). Thus, it is as if the murli point contains the entire treasure, including the entire tree of knowledge, that is within

God. The entire tree of knowledge is an expansion that is merged within that seed. Therefore, thinking on just one murli point enables you to understand any aspect of the knowledge that is amongst the treasure of knowledge within God. Further, since Baba is knowledge-full, every solution to your problems can be found in the Murli and these solutions can be used to live your life well in the human world tree.

Keep remembering that you are fortunate to have found God/Baba, the knowledge-full Seed of the human world tree. Keep thinking about how the new world tree is brought in through the knowledge-full Seed (God). All these will help you to experience God/Baba as the knowledge-full Seed of the human world tree. When the Seed is known, the knowledge about his creation (the world tree) is also known.

24   CHURNING THE JEWELS OF KNOWLEDGE

Murli Extract (SM 24-12-2018):

"A soul is a star; it resides in the centre of the forehead. ...God speaks: God is the Supreme Soul. He too is called a star. ...He is incorporeal. ...Everyone has a soul. Therefore, souls would surely have the Father who is called the Supreme Father, the Supreme Soul. All of these are points. By churning these, you will constantly find new points. The steamer will continue to be filled. This is like the goods of the imperishable jewels of knowledge. Note down the points and then revise them. These are jewels. You should have a keen interest in imbibing them and writing about them."

Churning:

The knowledge which God gives, during the Confluence Age, is imperishable because it is always there within Him. When you churn on murli points (the imperishable jewels of knowledge) in respect of the soul and Supreme Soul, you get linked to God. Hence, God places new points within your mind and you will have a better understanding of the knowledge. To easily receive such points, you must have the view that God is your Teacher and make spiritual efforts to experience the stage of being an embodiment; you have to absorb/imbibe the knowledge to become soul conscious and an embodiment of knowledge. When you attain the incorporeal stage, you get connected to the knowledge that always exists within God and so you are an embodiment of knowledge. In addition, while you are making spiritual efforts, God will be guiding and helping you to understand the knowledge.

Through contemplating on the murli points (imperishable jewels of knowledge), you receive something great and wonderful that can be enjoyed now and during the first half cycle. You enjoy the benefits until the end of the Silver Age. Then, your worship worthy form is worshipped until the end of the cycle. The worship worthy form is a memorial of what had happened during the Confluence Age, through which the divine world of the deities was created. At the end of the cycle, the deity souls use the knowledge again because the soul knows that a lot of benefits can be enjoyed through contemplating on it. In this way, the imperishable jewels of knowledge keep getting used at the end of each cycle. The knowledge is also imperishable in this sense. Since the soul enjoys the benefits, the soul would view the knowledge as jewels (valuable); hence the person would appreciate the knowledge. The knowledge is also valuable because the deep secrets of God and the Universe are revealed, and the ignorance of darkness is expelled.

When I was introduced to the BK knowledge and meditation in 1994, I felt that the knowledge and meditation were so wonderful like amrit/nectar. I, the soul, had been touched and so I (the person) was responding in a positive way. I formed the view that there is no other knowledge that is as brilliant as this knowledge. For me, remembering God is the most wonderful thing in the world. Nothing is greater than keeping God's Company. Due to remembering Him and the knowledge which He has given, I keep getting filled with more points and my understanding has improved.

While you are in God's Company, you would be subtly seeing God and interacting with Him. Some remember these interactions while others do not. Those who do not remember their experiences will only remember experiencing the blissful stage since they will continue to enjoy this stage for some time. Due to having such wonderful experiences, you would surely think that the knowledge is superb and would want to continue thinking intensely about it so that you can have more of such experiences. During these experiences, God would be placing more points in your mind and you would understand the knowledge to a greater extent. This helps you to have greater faith in God and the knowledge which He has given. It will also help you to maintain your stage of being an embodiment of knowledge.

To become an embodiment of knowledge you must have a **powerful link** to God. You can have such a powerful link to God through **constantly and intensely** churning on the knowledge which is in the Murli. Just as a diver dives deep into an ocean to acquire valuable pearls and other gems, the soul has to dive deep into the Ocean of Knowledge (God) to get the valuable jewels of knowledge. When you get it, it will be there in your mind.

If you do not churn the knowledge to become an embodiment of knowledge, God's treasure will not become your treasure. You do not gain experiences and you remain empty. You will also not get filled with God's Virtues and Powers. When you are not filled with God's Virtues and Powers, there is ample space for waste and negative thoughts to arise and occupy your mind. You yourself have provided this space for waste and negative thoughts to occupy since you were not contemplating on the knowledge that has been given by God. Instead of getting filled with waste, fill yourself up with murli points and God will fill your mind up with more points. This helps you to become, and remain as, an embodiment of knowledge.

To make sure that you become an embodiment when you contemplate on the jewels of knowledge, make sure that you belief that God has given the jewels of knowledge and that God has explained the truth. If you read the jewels of knowledge with doubts in your mind, you will not become an embodiment even though you will get some benefits. Constantly make spiritual efforts, with faith, so that you are a steamer that is continuously filled from the Ocean of Knowledge.

25   CONCLUSION

God/Baba has blessed us all with the ability to use the imperishable jewels of knowledge to become spiritually powerful. This means that you also have the ability to become spiritually powerful through churning this knowledge. It is just a matter of whether you churn this knowledge to enjoy the benefits. When churning the imperishable jewels of knowledge, you would be:

1. remembering that you are a soul.

2. remembering God.

3. remembering your experiences.

4. thinking about all aspects of the BK knowledge.

5. remembering what you have churned earlier on.

When you create thoughts based on the knowledge that has been given by God, you are also remembering

Him because He is the Source of the knowledge. The 'knowledge in the Murli' is like food or a shower for the soul. Just as we shower and consume food every day to keep our body healthy and free from diseases, the knowledge is also essential to keep the soul healthy and free from *vices and negative/waste thoughts*. Your new thinking process should only revolve around the imperishable jewels of knowledge because this will help you to become completely pure and divine, while you also enjoy a spiritually powerful stage now. Though this requires time, diligence and patience, it will be worth your while because as a consequence:

1. you will enjoy a feeling of abundance and magnificence since you are with God.

2. you will receive God's help and guidance. You get filled with wisdom, divine virtues and powers; these will be reflected through what you say and do.

3. life will flow well now when you are in high spiritual stage. You will flow along with the ups and downs with grace and ease since you are a detached observer.

4. you will become a brilliantly shining divine star. Hence, you can take births, in the heavenly Golden Aged world, as a world emperor.

Each moment in your life can be used beneficially to receive multimillion-fold benefits. So use your time and thinking process wisely. Don't say that you don't have time. Make sure that you do not have attachment to your old wasteful thinking process. God, our Father and Supreme Teacher, is teaching us how to think so that we transform into deities. You can claim an **imperishable status** from the eternal Father through using His teachings; what you claim now, will be retained within you (the soul) until the end of the Silver Age. So transform your thinking process for your own benefit; become a Raja Yogi through using this thinking process.

GLOSSARY

A

Adi Sanatan Devi Devta Dharma: the Original Eternal Deity Religion. The deities live a divine peaceful life-style, during the Golden and Silver Ages, since peace is the original religion of the soul and the deities are soul conscious.

Almighty Authority: Almighty God, the One who has all powers to remain as an authority and who is an authority on the knowledge.

AM: Avyakt Murli.

angelic body: the subtle body which we use in the Angelic World.

Angelic World: the Confluence Aged subtle region which is beyond the present Corporeal World.

avyakt: subtle, angelic, non-physical.

Avyakt Murli: the Murli which was given by BapDada through the physical body of Dadi Gulzar.

B

Baba: father.

bandhan: bondage.

Bap: father.

BapDada: the Supreme Soul playing His role together with Brahma Baba; the combined form of God and Brahma Baba.

Bestower of Happiness: God, our Father, who bestows us with happiness.

BK knowledge: the knowledge in the Murli which is used by the members of the Brahma Kumaris to create elevated thoughts.

bodiless stage: the spiritually high stage where one is aware that one is the soul and not the physical body. While in this stage, the soul is a detached observer.

body-conscious: the weak ordinary state.

Brahma: one who is involved with the creation of the Golden Aged world during the Confluence Age.

Brahma Baba: the founder of the Brahma Kumaris.

Brahmapuri: the place of residence of Brahma in the Confluence Aged subtle region.

Brahmin: those who were born via the knowledge given by God through the mouth of Brahma Baba (the chariot of God); one who is close to God during the Confluence Age.

C

canopy of protection: God's energies, which fill us through our link to God, provide us with a canopy of protection.

churn: to think deeply on the knowledge given by God in the Murli so as to have a full understanding of it and to have blissful experiences. We receive these benefits through the churning process, just as we get butter when the milk is churned.

Confluence Age: Sangamyug, the final age in the Cycle of Time which is after the Iron Age (Kaliyug).

controlling power: one's ability to have control over one's mind, intellect and sanskars.

Copper Age: the third age in the Cycle of Time which follows the Silver Age.

Cycle of Time (cycle): time repeats in a cyclic manner through 5 ages: Golden Age, Silver Age, Copper Age, Iron Age (Kaliyug) and Confluence Age.

D

Dada: grandfather, elder brother. Brahma Baba is our elder brother (when Shiv Baba is seen as our Father), and Shiv Baba is our grandfather (when Brahma Baba is seen as our spiritual/avyakt father).

deities: the human beings who live in the Golden and Silver Ages.

detached observer: one who observes everything in a detached manner without being influenced by what is perceived. One is soul conscious when one is a detached observer.

dharma: religion, way of life, code of conduct.

divine intellect: the intellect in the transformed divine state when we are in a high spiritually powerful stage. This divine intellect can be used to make quick, accurate decisions based on the spiritual knowledge and guidance from God.

E

embodiment of the essence: soul conscious stage.

embodiment of knowledge: the high spiritual stage when one is filled with knowledge.

G

gyan: the knowledge which is revealed by the Supreme Soul (God).

God's Sounds of Silence: God's vibrations which accompany the knowledge given by Him.

Golden Age: the first heavenly age in the Cycle of Time.

H

human world tree: this portrays what happens in the World Drama throughout the Cycle of Time.

I

imbibe: absorb.

incorporeal stage: the soul conscious stage; the stage where one experiences oneself as the pure powerful soul.

intellect: the power/faculty of the soul that is used to decide, etc.

Iron Age: Kaliyuga, the fourth age in the Cycle of Time

which follows the Copper Age.

K

Kaliyug/Kaliyuga: the darkest age in the Cycle of Time which is followed by Sangamyug (Confluence Age).

karma: action.

karma bandhan / karm bandhan: bondage of karma. Karmic bondages are created when actions are done during the weak state, when there is attachment to someone, etc.

karma yoga / karm yoga: remembrance of God whilst doing karma, i.e. having yoga with God whilst carrying out actions.

karmic accounts: bad accounts, created through the Law of Karma, which needs to be settled.

L

Laksmi: the deity who is the world empress in the Golden Age. During the Confluence Age, we can have experiences of being Lakshmi while we are in the subtle region. One is in a high divine stage during such experiences.

Land of Happiness: the Golden Aged world.

Land of Peace: the Soul World which is the supreme home of God and all human souls.

Law of Karma: the spiritual laws based on which we receive the fruits of our actions.

Liberator: God, our Father, who liberates us from sorrow.

lokik: worldly, physical.

lokik father: worldly father; father of the physical body.

M

Madhuban: Forest of Honey. The place where God meets His children at Mount Abu, India.

mantra: something that is constantly repeated.

master almighty authority: the powerful stage where one has all powers and one knows that the knowledge given by God, in the Murlis, is true.

Maya: the female demon representing the vices at the thought level, i.e. when actions are not taken, based on the thoughts, through using the physical body. Maya includes all waste/negative thoughts, memories of sinful actions which disturb the person and all other impure thoughts that get created due to the influence of the vices.

Maya-Ravan: the five vices influencing us to indulge in the *vices and negative/waste thinking*.

masters of heaven: the deities who live in the Golden Age.

memory bank: the faculty of the soul where all the memories are stored.

mind: the thinking faculty of the human soul.

Murli: the magic flute (God's teachings in the Brahma Kumaris) which brings us into a high spiritually intoxicating stage.

murli extract: an extract from one of the murlis.

N

Narayan: the deity who is the world emperor in the Golden Age. During the Confluence Age, we can have powerful experiences of being Narayan in Vishnupuri.

O

Ocean of Knowledge: God, the One who is filled with unlimited imperishable knowledge.

Ocean of Love: God, the One who is filled with unlimited Love.

Ocean of Peace: God, the One who is filled with unlimited Peace.

Ocean of Virtues and Powers: God, the One who is filled with unlimited virtues and powers.

Om: "I, the soul".

shanti: peace.

Om Shanti: "I, the soul, am an embodiment of peace" or "I am a peaceful soul".

Original Eternal Deity Religion: Adi Sanatan Devi Devta Dharma. The Original Eternal Deity Religion is also referred to as the Deity Religion for short. The deities, during the Golden and Silver Ages, live a pure divine peaceful life-style because they are constantly and naturally soul conscious.

original religion: peace is the original religion of the soul.

P

Paramdham: the Soul World which is the supreme Home of God and all human souls.

Parlokik Father: God, the One who is our spiritual father or the One who is our Father from beyond. He is the Father from Parlok (Soul World).

Parvati: the wife of Shiva/God. During the Confluence Age, we are the wives of Shiva/God.

Purifier: God, the One who purifies the human souls. Only Baba/God is the Purifier. During the purification process, one's sins get burnt away and the energies of the soul get transformed into the pure state.

power of concentration: the ability/power to concentrate on something for a long period of time.

power of coolness: the spiritually high cool stage which one uses as a power to keep the thoughts, words and others cool.

power of discernment: the ability/power to use the intellect to make decisions.

R

raja: king.

Raja Yoga: the highest form of yoga through which we become self-sovereigns now and sovereigns in the Golden Age.

Raja Yogi: a self-sovereign; one who is a king in respect of one's own mind, intellect, sanskaras and sense organs.

Ravan/Ravana: the demon king representing the five vices: anger, lust, greed, attachment and ego. The personification of the 'five vices in a man and five vices in a woman', i.e. the devilish king (demon) with ten heads.

Remover of Sorrow: God, our Father, who removes all our sorrow through the purification process.

ruling power: the ability/power to rule over the 3 powers (mind, intellect and sanskaras) when one has control over these 3 powers.

S

sakar: the physical form.

Sakar Murli: the Murli which was given by God through using the physical body of Brahma Baba.

Sangamyug: the final age in the Cycle of Time which follows Kaliyug.

sanskara: an impression on the energies of the soul which becomes a memory or latent tendency within the soul.

sanskaras: the memory bank, within the soul, where all the memories are stored.

Satguru: God, the preceptor/teacher, who is the True Guru. Only God can be the Satguru because only He speaks the truth.

self-sovereign: the state where the soul is a king within the body, i.e. in control of the sense organs and subtle powers (mind, intellect, sanskaras) which are within its kingdom (within the soul and body).

service: selfless actions which spread God's message to all and which help to transform the world into the Golden Aged world.

Shankar: a subtle deity in the Confluence Aged subtle region. The highest Confluence Aged stage is the Shankar stage.

Shankarpuri: the place of residence of Shanker in the Confluence Aged subtle region.

shanti: peace.

Shiva: God's name which means "a Point", "World Benefactor", "the Seed of the Human World Tree", etc. God comes and introduces Himself through using this name.

Shiv Baba: God Shiva, our Father. Shiv Baba is our parlokik Father; He is the imperishable spiritual Father of the imperishable souls.

shrimat: God's directions which are given through the murlis.

Silver Age: the second age in the Cycle of Time which follows the Golden Age.

SM: Sakar Murli.

soul: a metaphysical point of living white light.

soul conscious: the powerful stage where one knows that one is the soul and not the physical body. While in this stage, one experiences the original qualities of the soul and uses them, while carrying out activities, since one is seated on one's seat in the center of the forehead.

Soul World: the supreme abode of God and all human souls.

spinner of the discus of self-realisation: one who contemplates on how one's state changes as the soul continues to take rebirths in the world drama cycle (from the Golden Age to the end of the Iron Age), and one also ruminates on how God comes and uplifts the soul during the Confluence Age. Also known as Swadarshanchakradhari.

spiritual income: the spiritual benefits earned, through spiritual effort making, via the Law of Karma.

Supreme Soul: God who is a metaphysical Point of White Light.

swadarshan chakra: discus of self-realization. This symbolises that *one has the awareness of how one's stage changes in the world drama cycle*; "swa" means I, "darshan" means see or knowledge and "chakra" refers to the cycle.

Swadarshanchakradhari: spinner of the discus of self-realisation.

T

tapasya: intense, very powerful yoga/meditation through renunciation; the surrendered, self-disciplined/austere, non-worldly, intense meditative stage of Shankar.

trilokinath: lord of the three worlds (incorporeal Soul

World, Angelic World and Corporeal World). BKs are lords of the three worlds since they know the three worlds.

trimurti powers: mind, intellect and sanskaras. The soul uses these three powers while living its life.

V

Vishnu: this is a four-armed deity who symbolises the perfect couple of the pure divine family path that exists during the Golden Age. Vishnu represents the combined form of the Golden Aged Lakshmi and Narayan who sustain the Golden Aged world. During the Confluence Age, we can have powerful experiences of being Vishnu in Vishnupuri.

Vishnupuri: the place of residence of Vishnu, Lakshmi and Narayan in the Confluence Aged subtle region.

visualization: creation of thoughts through using images.

W

waste thoughts: thoughts which are not beneficial.

world tree: this reflects what happens in the World Drama throughout the Cycle of Time; it portrays what happens in each religion too as the world drama continues to take place on earth.

Y

yoga: union, link or connection. Sitting in remembrance and having a link to God, our Father, who is the Supreme Soul.

yogi: one who practices yoga.

Om Shanti

Made in the USA
Middletown, DE
01 May 2023